In and Out of Anorexia

of related interest

Anorexics on Anorexia
Edited by Rosemary Shelley
ISBN 1 85302 471 6

A Systemic Treatment of Bulimia Nervosa
Women in Transition
Carole Kayrooz
ISBN 1 85302 918 1

Bulimia Nervosa
A Cognitive Therapy Programme for Clients
Myra Cooper, Gillian Todd and Adrian Wells
ISBN 1 85302 717 0

Figures of Lightness
Anorexia, Bulimia and Psychoanalysis
Gabriella Ripa di Meana
ISBN 1 85302 617 4

More Than Just a Meal
The Art of Eating Disorders
Susan R. Makin
Forewords by Bryan Lask and Cathy A. Malchiodi
ISBN 1 85302 805 3

Arts Therapies and Clients with Eating Disorders
Fragile Board
Edited by Ditty Dokter
ISBN 1 85302 256 X

Self-Mutilation and Art Therapy
Violent Creation
Diana Milia
ISBN 1 85302 683 2

In and Out of Anorexia

The Story of the Client, the Therapist and the Process of Recovery

Tammie Ronen and Ayelet

Jessica Kingsley Publishers
London and Philadelphia

First published in the United Kingdom in 2001 by
Jessica Kingsley Publishers Ltd
116 Pentonville Road
London N1 9JB, England
and
325 Chestnut Street
Philadelphia, PA 19106, USA

www.jkp.com

Library of Congress Cataloging in Publication Data
A CIP catalog record for this book is available from the Library of Congress

British Library Cataloguing in Publication Data
A CIP catalogue record for this book is available from the British Library

ISBN 1 85302 990 4

Printed and Bound in Great Britain by
Athenaeum Press, Gateshead, Tyne and Wear

Contents

I. *Ayelet's Story: On Becoming Anorexic*

List of Illustrations

To our husbands, who were very much involved in the process of writing, and who supported and challenged us to undertake this project; and to our children, who inspired our writing before and after being born.

Tammie and Ayelet

Acknowledgement

I wish to express my deepest gratitude to Dee B. Ankonina, who has stood alongside me since the beginning of my professional journey – at first only as my editor and then later as a partner in our thinking processes, experiences, and writing. Dee has become a source of support, and a real friend over the years. For all this, I thank her.

Tammie Ronen

Before We Begin
An Overview

We are sitting in the garden, a beautiful tall young woman in her 20s, and an older woman in her 40s. Near each of us there is a little four-month-old baby. We are talking, smiling, and, every so often, leaning toward our infants. A stranger passing by would be impressed by the obviously close friendship between these two women 20 years apart in age. Almost a generation apart, yet we do not feel a gap. We share significant common experiences – of recently being pregnant and having a child. But also, we share many similarities in how we think, look at events, analyze things, demand the best from ourselves and from others we care about, and enjoy our creativity. No one can tell that these two women are, or actually, were, a client and a therapist. Certainly, no one can tell that the younger woman had been hospitalized many times, for many months, because of anorexia, depression, and severely self-destructive behavior.

It is strange what life brings us. An Old Jewish (Yiddish) saying asserts: 'Man plans and God laughs.' I never planned to become involved in the formidable therapeutic encounter with Ayelet, and, in fact, I even tried to avoid it. For many years during Ayelet's adolescence, her parents had unsuccessfully tried to persuade me to treat her. Afraid of the enormous responsibility involved and of the possible need to deal with recurrent hospitalizations, I declined. I thought that a private therapist in a private clinic should not treat a girl with such severe problems. Eventually, however, after the parents came to me with Ayelet and I had a chance to meet her, I reluctantly agreed to undertake her treatment. Something about Ayelet drew me to her and allowed me to take the risk, to walk into the unknown. Upon meeting her and hearing her story, I realized that I did have the potential to help her, and that I wanted to embark on this challenging journey together with her.

No one could predict that treating Ayelet would become such a special experience for the two of us. No one could predict that not only would Ayelet overcome all of her problems, but she would also become such a wonderful young woman. No one could predict that we would sit down to write a book together. Or that, in the process, we would share motherhood experiences and even become good friends.

This book was born in one of our last therapeutic meetings. Ayelet presented me with an album of all her writings and drawings from the time of her hospitalizations. The first page was dedicated to me:

> *You knew me in good hours and in my most difficult ones*
> *You saw me in sorrow and watched me overcome*
> *You listened to me whether I was talking foolishness or making sense*
> *You were with me in deep sorrow and at times of happiness*
> *You watched me as I cried and as I laughed*
> *You understood me behaving or misbehaving*
> *My thanks to you for your patience while I cried over my past*
> *My thanks to you for your support, your love, and your unconditional*
>   *trust*
> *For your readiness to walk beside me always*
> *And for teaching me to discover the young woman inside me*
> *My thanks are not for what you did*
> *But for who you are*
> *Not for one specific thing*
> *But for everything…*

I read her poem and excitedly told her I thought she could publish it. Several weeks later, Ayelet told me that in order to achieve closure regarding the previous chapter in her life, she felt compelled to write her own story. She asked me if I would join her in the writing process. I hesitated. I didn't want her to expose herself. We live in Israel – a small country where everyone knows one another. I wasn't sure that her story wouldn't damage her future career as a teacher. I didn't know if Ayelet was ready for the inevitable publicity that such a book would bring in our local landscape. Although I was convinced that the writing endeavor itself could be extremely beneficial and rewarding for Ayelet, I was still concerned as to how she would handle the experience of people talking about her, both in close circles and possibly in the local media. I persuaded her to abandon the idea.

A few years later, Ayelet again proposed to me that we write her story together. In the interim, she had married and had recently given birth to her first child. We had maintained contact over the years. I had enjoyed watching her blossom and find a sense of peace within herself, as a wife and now as a new mother. Feeling that she could now cope with whatever the book would evoke, I agreed to collaborate with her on this initiative. However, I suggested that we first publish it overseas to avoid the intense exposure of a local Hebrew language press, and here we are.

I thought that this book would mean the end of our relationship, but, actually, it constituted only the beginning of a wonderful friendship. My clinic is in the basement of the house. Until we started working on the book, Ayelet used to enter the house through the separate clinic entrance. As we began meeting to write together, she came into my home, my living room, and my life. I didn't realize then, at the outset, that writing this book would be such a demanding task and would open up so many new directions of thought, discussion, and clarification, while arousing so many emotions. It proved to be a very exhilarative process for both of us. It seemed, at times, that talking about therapy was more therapeutic than the therapy itself.

I know now that this book is not the end of a story but the beginning. I know that I, too, have much for which to thank Ayelet. I have learned immensely from her as a therapist and as a human being.

Before beginning the book, I want to share with our readers a bit about what I believe has been a unique and productive writing process. This process generated what I consider to be some remarkably meaningful insights articulated by Ayelet, and also elicited my disclosure of some of my own deep experiences as her therapist.

As Ayelet and I began planning and talking about our book, we found ourselves interviewing each other about the treatment. I also started asking Ayelet questions about the ensuing period and about her current feelings as a wife and mother and in her career. I wanted to know how she views herself now, and how she looks back at her past as an anorexic.

Ayelet said that her life, now, is too important to endanger. 'I love my husband and my baby. I want to give and share with them, and to be with them. But I won't lie to you. The thoughts still exist. I still think about how I should lose weight, and how I look better being thin. The difference is that now, when I have those thoughts, I know they're irrational, and I also know that I won't do anything about them. In the past, having such thoughts would have made me start dieting immediately.' Looking back, Ayelet was able to describe her previous satisfaction from pain itself, while starving or while trying to commit suicide, in terms of sadistic enjoyment. In our recent talks, she emphasized repeatedly that she would never do those things again, even if occasionally such thoughts do pass through her mind.

I asked her if she could now explain the reasons for what happened to her, and she gave several. She first emphasized her family relations, viewing her anorexia as something that compelled her parents to unite in order to help her, thus enabling them to ignore their own problems. 'I think my parents had some real problems. They also thought people should never express negative feelings. Maybe my anorexia made it possible for them to ignore their difficulties. They focused all their efforts, arguments, and discussions on trying to help me recover. That way, my problem forced them to talk, be together, and maybe even stay together. I gave them an excuse to continue the way they were living.'

Another reason Ayelet provided was related to her symbiotic relationship with her mother, and the need to take an extreme step in order to disconnect that relationship: 'I think my mother was more dependent on me than I was on her. Even recently, she wanted us to study together for a teaching certification. I think there was too close a relationship between the two of us.'

Listening to Ayelet, it was as if she had read all the theories. She talked about early attachment, without knowing the professional concepts. She told me she was born prematurely and was left for a month in the hospital. Her mother did not take care of her for many weeks until she came home.

Last, she gave some personal reasons for the anorexia. First, she talked about eating problems that she had had since birth, relating how her mother used to force her to eat. She then described some fears of sexuality and development and her wish to remain a child.

Clearly, Ayelet is a very intelligent young woman. Although she said she did not read about anorexia, I am sure her multiple treatments and many years spent among anorexic girls taught her a great deal about anorexia. One should remember that she is talking about herself from the perspective of a healthy, grown up, college graduate looking back at herself as a sick child.

On the one hand, it is interesting to see her understanding, her insight, and her sensitivity as a mature, healthy young woman. On the other hand, even as we began writing the book, I was once again struck by how Ayelet talked about her problems. She used very poetic language, rich metaphors, and colorful words; yet, as she spoke, she seemed to be far away. Even now, after all these years, Ayelet talks about herself as if she were another person. Her words are full of pain, but her emotion does not come through. Her voice does not betray the slightest change in tone. In our sessions, she always aroused in me a great deal of concern and caring, but at the same time Ayelet always kept me away. She never cried. Detached, uninvolved, it was as if she was holding up a stop sign, saying: 'Don't come any closer.' In telling her story, I have attempted to remain as faithful as possible to the truth. I tried to convey this voice of pain yet coldness and detachment – her ambivalent tendency to let someone in but also to keep her distance.

During our writing and mutual interviewing process, Ayelet asked me questions as well. She was eager to know what made me agree to treat her. I admitted that I was intimidated by the long list of previous medications, prior therapists, and hospitalizations. I told her about a few times that I had regretted accepting her to my clinic. I admitted that, at times, I lost sleep at night fearing that something would happen to her. I told her about the time I was debating about whether I should hospitalize her again. About how I was wondering if her life was at real risk, if she was being honest with me, etc.

Our talks would have lasted uninterrupted for hours, if not for our two babies calling for our attention. Ayelet would get up and go home, leaving me with the feeling that writing this book was a kind of spiritual experience for me. The writing was, in a way, only an excuse to get close to this unique human being. To strengthen our relationship, and to gain understanding about the long road we had traveled together.

And, now, let me introduce the content and process of this book: The two of us wrote the large majority of this book, together. The way we worked was by meeting every week and holding discussions. I interviewed Ayelet, asking her to remember different aspects and times. I tried to structure her complicated story.

This book is divided into three sections. The first section (Parts I and III) portrays Ayelet's own story of her life, her illness, and her therapy. I recorded her account, trying to preserve her language and her way of relating to issues while translating it into English. Ayelet has a very picturesque language and a remarkably creative way of thinking. During translation, I tried to keep the story as close as possible to the way it was told to me in Hebrew. I only changed words to organize the sequence. The written materials as well as the drawings are hers — with my translation. I checked and rechecked everything with Ayelet. We both approved each word that was written.

The second section (Part II) comprises my own account of the treatment. I wrote it while Ayelet sat next to me, adding things, commenting, asking questions, or arguing at times. In places, she asked me to add what she felt or did in the sessions. Thus, this part is written in first-person language, in my voice, but in actuality is a joint product.

The third section (Parts IV, V, and VI) provides a theoretical backdrop to the preceding personal stories and clinical encounters. In this part, I summarize the literature about anorexia, present my therapeutic approach as influenced by the self-control and cognitive-constructivist modes of intervention, and provide guidelines for therapists. In order to facilitate teenagers', parents', and teachers' understanding of professional terms, a glossary has been provided at the end of this book. Other than this introduction, only these parts of the book were written solely by me.

I hope this book will be helpful to mental health professionals, including hospital staff and private clinicians, but, at the same time, this book unequivocally reaches out to young women suffering from similar problems as well as to their parents and other family members. I hope even school counselors and pediatricians can learn from this volume more about the hope underlying the heartache of anorexia. I have had as my ultimate aim the need to treat Ayelet the person — not her problem. I hope I have succeeded also in conveying our thoughts and mutual emotions in the process.

Tammie Ronen
Tel Aviv

PART I

Ayelet's Story

On Becoming Anorexic

I

Introduction

Was I Ever a Normal Child?

People who knew me as a child, as well as those who met me later on, throughout my years at university or as I started working as a teacher, keep wondering: Could it be true? Could it be that a charming, intelligent, pretty, smart person like me was hospitalized because of anorexia, actually wished to die, and spent most of her adolescence away from the world? Knowing myself now, I also sometimes wonder. Was that really me who experienced all those horrible things? How could I have survived it and stayed sane? Have I changed? Am I a different person?

Some people look back at a difficult time and say: 'That wasn't me. I can't recognize myself.' But to be honest, I can't say that. So much is still the same. I am the same person, with the same thoughts and emotions. But I am older and smarter, and I suffer less. I can see the first signs of my disorder in myself as early as when I was a small child. From where I stand now, a so-called normal healthy woman, looking back at the process of how my anorexia developed, I can almost say that it was inevitable, that it had to be. It was a natural process. Natural? Not for everyone, but for me, yes. A natural outgrowth from where I was, from the way I was raised, and from how I developed. When I look at the worst time in my life – in the hospitals – I don't see that any new, unexpected behaviors or emotions suddenly appeared as if by magic. Rather, I can see all those parts of me that had been slowly growing since birth. Who could have known then that they would turn into anorexia?

Yet, as I look at myself now, I must admit that nothing has actually changed. I can't really say that I'm a different person today than that girl in the hospital or that child before her. I am the same me. The same person, with the same internal doubts, suspicions, emotions, and thoughts. Still struggling and coping with the same issues. But how can I say that nothing has changed? Then how is it possible that today I'm a happy wife, mother, and human being? Me – the expert in suffering and pain. The miserable soul. How can it be that I'm normal? Am I recovered?

I think I know. Yes, it is the same me, the same person, the same inner materials, the same doubts. However, my perspective about the world is different now. Along the way, in all my suffering, I made a detour, acquired a new perspective, and learned to trust and care for myself, not only for others. I have learned to redefine my pain, and to express my emotions differently, but what has changed the most is my behavior. My basic thoughts remain similar to what they were in the past – I've only labeled them differently. I continue to be overly self-critical, checking and rechecking myself. My emotions are still very complex, still encompassing a lot of ambivalence, sometimes fears, and always the need to be accepted by others. It's true that some of my emotions are different now: I also have happiness, fun, exciting feelings – and I've learned to accept all of them as a normal, healthy part of my life.

My behavior is what has changed the most. I certainly no longer act the same. Now, when I sometimes get those same thoughts and feelings – about the world, myself, evil, and fears – I can tell myself that I should never act the way I used to. And I know that I will not regress. I know that I will not be hospitalized again. I will never harm myself again.

I know now that my old way of looking at the world – the dichotomous view of good and bad, of right and wrong – does not exist. I wasn't only bad, so I couldn't become only good. Each of us is a combination of things. Now I can also accept that I am a good human being who has the right to live.

At 25 years of age, with a history of 7 years of anorexia, about 12 therapists, 24 different kinds of medications, and 5 different hospitalizations in 5 different kinds of hospitals, I am still not sure what was wrong. Were the hospitalizations and treatments essential? Where did my problems lie – in family, society, or me? Could I have become me, the person I am today, without being hospitalized? Perhaps I would have been a better person. Who knows? Maybe it was just meant to be. Maybe it was a kind of catharsis. A mind-clearing, crystallizing process that discarded all the bad within me, and then let me start living again, as a better person.

Sometimes I wonder: Was I conceived with these problems? Now that I've become a mother myself, I've become sensitive to my baby son and what he has been experiencing throughout the pregnancy. I believe that even before being born we feel things. We are aware of the world around us. I am sure my baby knew how happy and anxious we were for him to come into the world. Was I aware of the world before being born? Did I know about my parents' fears, anxieties, and ambivalent emotions? Did I feel neglected or afraid while alone in the incubator? I have no idea.

I don't know how to explain the fact that I changed but actually remained the same person. Maybe I just learned to accept myself and live with myself. Maybe what I learned most was to make peace with my soul, and with my environment. I feel good, and I enjoy life. Sometimes the thoughts do come back. Is it because thoughts are harder to change than behaviors? Is it because they are too deeply fixed within me to be changed? Is it because I want to keep something of the old me? Often, I start thinking and rethinking, trying once again to understand: Why do I have these problems, and who is responsible for them? It is true that each person is responsible for his or her own life, and for whatever meaning he or she imposes onto it. Does that imply that I, and only I, am responsible for the development of my anorexia? Yet, at the same time, it's also true that we have an inherited set of behaviors deep inside us. So, does that mean that I inherited my anorexia? Are my family history and genes responsible?

What's responsible for my disorder – what I inherited or what I created out of my life? I guess I'll never know the answers to that, and the truth is, although I've pondered them more while writing this book, they don't weigh me down in the routine of my life.

And I have a good life now. I'm happy. In fact, it's the happiest time in my entire life. I love my husband, my children, and I can even say that I love myself. I love my husband, who shares all my difficulties with me. We both adore our baby son, and we know we will raise him with lots of love, trust, and confidence. I am not even afraid that he'll develop my disorders. How do I have this security? I don't know, but something is going very right for me lately. (Tammie would probably say: 'It's not going right for you. You're the one who makes it go right for yourself. It's not by chance – it's where you lead things. You control yourself and your world. You are doing and acting right for yourself.') And I believe in my love and my wish to nurture my son. With love and caring, and with my husband's help, I know I can.

I even feel very happy with my relationships with my two sisters and my parents. For many years, I had such complicated relationships with them, especially with my older sister. I used to envy her and compete with her, but now she has become a good friend. My younger sister has grown up. I always felt lots of affection toward her, but she was young. She wasn't a part of my life, of my growing up, of my suffering. She was too young to share feelings with. Now that she's matured, now that she's started asking questions and has become curious and interested, we've become closer.

With my parents, it's a different story. I was not an easy child. It was not easy for them to see all that I went through. I always challenged their love, their understanding, their trust. It was not easy for all of us to experience what we did over the years. Now, as a mother, I can appreciate how difficult it was for them to deal with my sickness, and what they've gone through. For many years, I blamed them for the way they behaved. I hope our closer relationship now will help them understand that it was part of my sickness that caused this blaming and accusing. I looked at myself as a bad human being and I saw everyone around me as bad, too. Naturally, my parents were also included in that tendency of mine to view everything as bad. I hope my children will not challenge me and will not force me to experience all the things I made my parents experience. I don't know if I could bear it. I think it would be terrible.

Now, I am happy I have my parents. They are terrific grandparents, and we get along wonderfully. I deeply hope that my mother and my father – who both used to try so hard to hide things – will not be offended by my book. I hope they understand that all the things I say about them in this book relate not to the absolute truth, but rather to what I felt with and lived with then. I love them, and I appreciate them. I am sorry if telling my story will cause them sorrow or pain. But I feel I have to tell the truth, and my truth includes my ambivalent feelings toward them, my anger and my criticism.

Why am I writing this book? Several years ago, I told Tammie of my wish to do so. She tried to change my decision, fearing that it might harm me to expose myself to the public. But I am stronger now, and feel the need to do this. Part of it is that I'm learning to understand myself better via the writing process. Part of my motivation is a yearning to complete the story. Ending the unfinished journey of my growing up and maturing. Finishing unfinished business. I feel I have to do this in order to leave my sickness far behind me. And another part of my motivation is to help the world understand. I have been treated by so many people, and many of them didn't really change anything in me or for me. What I felt then was that they didn't really care about my real spirit. I know it was very complicated, but I felt that they never stepped back to take a look beyond all the mess and to find me, to see me. I hope I will succeed in conveying what I feel. And I truly hope that this book will help people understand what we – anorexic girls – are going through. Maybe it will give some clues to therapists in making decisions about how to treat us. Maybe it will help parents understand their children better, or be more optimistic.

First, I will try to show what occurred throughout my life that influenced my sickness and my soul and behavior.

2

Childhood

Exploring the Roots of My Anorexia

I am not sure whether my conception was planned. I was the middle child, with one sister two years older and another sister eleven years younger. My mother was a kindergarten teacher and my father was in the army. I was born prematurely, in the seventh month, and weighed 4 pounds 3 ounces. There was no premature infant intensive care unit in the hospital where I was born. Therefore, I was transferred to another hospital in order to be hospitalized until I gained weight and was out of danger. I was transferred alone, without my parents. My father came to visit me every day, but I was treated and fed by the nurses. I was so small. My mother was not confident enough to take care of me, and she got scared and panicky whenever she saw me. My father, trying to protect my mother, did not tell her the truth about how fragile I was. He didn't want her to know that I continued losing weight and that my life was in danger. My father was the one to visit me every day, and he informed my mother about my condition to the extent he felt she could handle. I stayed at that hospital for six weeks before I first came home. Sometimes I wonder: Can it be that, even as a very small infant, I felt neglected? Did I miss my mother's touch? Maybe there lie the roots of my insecure feelings and lack of confidence. Whenever I think of it, I keep hugging my child close, promising him and myself that such an experience will never happen to him!

If we believe that even a young infant knows and feels, if we believe that birth and the first few days are crucial for the child's development, then here we can see the beginning of the problem in early attachment between me and my mother. Maybe my father, who was more confident, was the one to send me early signals of trust and assurance, and his visits to the hospital might be part of the reasons for my very special relationship with him to this day. My relationships with my mother and my father are extremely complex, yet they differ. I know both of them love me a lot and would do anything for me. They are different kinds of people, with different personalities. There is a great contrast between them in how they think, live, and feel. This gap has been very obvious to me ever since I can remember. It always made me wonder who I should satisfy, which of the two ways to choose, and who was really my model. I can see now that I have inherited things from both of them. I am a blend of the two of them, and both of them have influenced my personality.

A child usually cannot look at his or her parents as complete personalities, as full human beings, something beyond just the parent figure. Usually children view their parents as a role model, worshipping them and thinking them perfect. Only when they start to mature during adolescence do children begin seeing their parents' deficiencies. Then they start accepting the fact that their parents are only human, like all the other people around.

For me, as for all other children, it was important to be appreciated by my parents, to be accepted by them, and to fulfill their expectations. I believe now that a major component of my disorders stemmed from my feeling that I was never good enough. I always felt I was not what my parents wished me to be. Unlike other children, I could not see my parents as perfect. I could see who they were and what I liked or disliked in them. But I blamed myself for seeing their deficiencies, instead of just understanding that they weren't perfect. As you will be able to read later on in my writings, I had the need to arrange my world in very clear concepts, and in a simple order. For me, things had to be either good or bad. I could not accept the fact that people are not only good or only bad, but are a combination of each. I was confused by trying to understand who is good and who is bad. I had to classify people in order to locate myself. So, I was always wondering and looking for explanations. Always trying to put order in my world. So, I'll try to explain who I am by, first of all, relating to my parents.

My Mother as a Role Model

My mother's most significant trait was, and still is, her sensitivity. Now, I can say that this sensitivity – her wonderful ability to express herself, to express emotions, and to understand emotions – is something I like and inherited. It's something I really enjoy and respect, and I consider it a very important characteristic. However, as an adolescent, it was hard for me to understand her behavior and emotions. Her sensitivity made me angry. Sometimes I'd get confused and want to run away from her. I always feared that her over-sensitivity would turn into anxiety. My mother is definitely a very anxious person. Her anxiety was something that disturbed me as far back as I can remember, and still continues to play a very important role in her life. She fears everything. She fears making mistakes, fears causing harm, fears not doing something right. I think that very fearfulness was already there when she was afraid to take care of me, when I was born. That's how I view the way she raised me, and that's how I see her now, with my child. She is afraid of feeding my son because she isn't sure how warm the food should be, what kind of bottle or amount of food he needs. She keeps complimenting me for being so brave while giving him a bath and for taking care of things that I see as very natural and don't give a second thought.

Her anxiety goes together with her over-protective behavior. It was that very combination of sensitivity and anxiety that always made her so over-protective of me. She always felt she needed to protect us from being hurt. Maybe she believes the world is dangerous and she needed to protect us and make sure we'd be safe. I have no idea why she is like that. I don't see these character traits in my grandparents. But I certainly inherited some of it. In a strange way, I made a shift in my mother's idea of the world as a dangerous place. I turned this view around. I always felt that *I* was dangerous for the world. Maybe part of my problems are related to the fact that I was an anxious child. I always wanted everyone to think I was good. I felt I needed to satisfy everyone, and I did not dare rebel. I always tried to comply with my parents' wishes (or with what I believed these were), even if I did not agree with them.

My mother's mixture of over-sensitivity and protectiveness interfered with her ability to educate me, use limits, be consistent, and be direct with me – all elements that I now understand to be crucially important in raising children. Even when my anorexia started developing, my mother found it difficult to insist that I eat normally or to make me go to therapy. For a long time, I took advantage of these difficulties that she had, and would do whatever I wanted. However, when she eventually realized how serious my condition was, she was so anxious that she did not even dare try to take care of me herself or treat me at home. Instead, she immediately agreed to my hospitalizations and accepted those doctors' diagnoses. Much later, that same anxiety also caused her to discharge me from the hospital, fearing that my soul would get lost there. Again, it is so hard to say when good things stop and bad things start. I love her sensitivity, I suffered from her anxiety, and I think what disturbed me most was her unexpected shift between the two. I could never know if she was going to care for me so as to hide me from the world, or if she was about to let the world take me away and treat me outside.

Another of my mother's traits is her perfectionism. This belongs to the same family of emotions as does sensitivity and anxiety. Her anxiety and over-protectiveness led her to perfectionism. Ever since I was a small child, I remember my mother as a very perfectionistic person. I saw it then in her very obsessive way of cleaning and her need to have everything around her be immaculate, a trait that I probably acquired from her. I think of this each time I change my son's clothes because they're spotted. Of course, her perfect way of doing things made many achievements possible for her, as clearly shown by her academic accomplishments. My mother recently started continuing her studies toward a university degree, and she's doing very well. In fact, because I just finished my bachelor's degree in special education, both of us are now working simultaneously for our teaching license, and we attend some similar courses. I can see her perfectionism clearly when she studies – she needs to read every possible thing and will not settle for less than the maximum. When I photocopied some course materials for her, she spent a lot of time checking and rechecking that I'd given her every single page, just in case the lecturer might ask her to read them.

These circumstances of studying together bring up the very complicated symbiotic relationship between me and my mother. My mother insists on taking the same courses I take; she wants us to study together and thinks it would be fun to learn together and share this experience. I don't want to hurt her, but I don't feel confident sitting with her in the same class. I'm happy to share materials or help her, but I don't want to see her among my friends. Is it because I'm afraid of not being the best? Is it my fear of competition? Anyway, I'm not sure it's good for the two of us. I never shared these feelings with her, and I hope she will not be angry while reading them in the book. Maybe it will open up a new opportunity for us to discuss our relationship. Because, as much as I criticize her, I have to admit that I really love her, care for her, and appreciate her. What a complex situation!

I both like and hate this perfectionism that I inherited from her. I know that perfectionism is what enabled me to receive good grades in school and to succeed in everything I did. Yet it also made me suffer from the gnawing need to always do things the right way, and from that ever-present fear of making mistakes. I always felt I had to be perfect, like her, in order to be appreciated. The truth is that she never asked me to follow her lead, but she was my role model for doing everything the right way. Ever since birth, I never settled for less than the best. If I wasn't good enough, then I considered myself to be very bad. This is a sentence you will probably be hearing from me a lot.

My perfectionism led me to tear up my drawings as a child. I never felt they were good enough, or as good as my sister's. I didn't want to settle for second best, so I'd get rid of them. It was the same with my grades in school – I had to be the first in class. And it's still the same now, as a wife and a mother – I still need to be perfect.

I guess it was the combination of perfectionism and anxiety that led me to constantly feel uncertain, to always hesitate, and to feel such a lack of confidence. My parents', and especially my mother's, great uncertainty and demand for flawlessness while raising me must have influenced me significantly. They loved me, but they often argued intensely about things and gave me double messages. My mother was never sure about how they should treat me as a child and, most of all, as an adolescent who needed to be hospitalized. I now can see my mother as a very weak woman. Today, she is very excited by the way we're raising her grandson. What guides us in raising our child is to behave naturally, trusting that our love will guide us to do the right thing, being sure that we will never do anything to harm him. But my parents did not have this trust and were always afraid of causing harm.

As I started dating my boyfriend, and later on became pregnant, I often talked with Tammie about my fears of harming my children. We tried to understand, together, what made me the same but also so different from my parents. We talked about what could reassure me that I would be able to raise children who would grow up normally. One of the things we discussed was the fact that my wish to do things right didn't make me anxious, as it did for my mother. Rather, it makes me eager to learn and to improve. But maybe the most important thing is that, in therapy, I have learned to trust myself. Instead of thinking of myself as an ex-hospitalized crazy person, I've learned to think of myself as a strong person who grew tremendously and improved as a result of my difficult experiences.

Growing up, I felt I always had to justify my actions in terms of what others would think of me. My life felt as if I was flowing along a river into which I had been thrown, without really having control. I sensed that I had to be on par with others, but I couldn't. I would always talk about me and them. I was the weak person who didn't know how to behave. They, on the other hand, were the world. The others. Those who knew what to do and how to do it right. This issue of feeling myself in contrast with those 'others' accompanied me for many years and was a main issue at the time I was hospitalized. Because the 'others' put me away, I felt they knew what they were doing; therefore, I had to act according to their expectations. I had to wear the image of the person they put in the pajamas, however remote from the real me. I often think about that time. Maybe it was a part of my search for a place where I could fit in, where I could be related to, a time of trying to be like others. Now that I've learned about early attachment, I can see how I did not have a trusting attachment, and perhaps that was why I was always looking over my shoulder, never confident, trusting, or sure of myself.

My Very Different Father

My relationship with my father was completely different from that with my mother. Young children usually start out by seeing their parents as one identity, as being the same: 'My parents want me to...' I could never say that, because they were so different from each other that I could never combine them into one parental unit. My father was much stronger. If I had to draw them, I would draw my father with his legs rooted firmly on the ground, and my mother would be flying in the sky. Many times, his strength reached the degree of rigidity. My father could not understand doubts, hesitations, or double messages. For him, to this day, things are very clear cut. His life is much more strict, simple, and clear than my mother's. He thinks in black and white and is not concerned by all the complex emotions that preoccupy her.

I was extremely aware of these incongruencies during my illness. For example, at that time my mother was preoccupied by trying to look at the significance of everything: 'What do they really mean when they say that Ayelet is in danger? Do you think she could die? Do you think she'll commit suicide? Will she become crazy? Does it mean we'll always have to look after her? I'm so afraid. What does the future hold?' My father, on the other hand, would accept everything as-is, without trying to look for hidden cues: 'Why don't you just wait and see? Ayelet is in good hands now; they will take care of her.' My mother would talk about 'accepting, fearing, being uncertain', while my father would suggest, 'Let's go get such and such for her.' She would talk about what I was feeling and experiencing, whereas he would talk about things I needed for him to bring me. He never expressed emotions. He talked about behavior.

I feel better with my father now. Maybe therapy helped him express emotions better, or maybe I've learned to read and understand his emotions better. I used to think that he lacked sensitivity, but now I think that he was just confused and overwhelmed by the amount of emotion that my mother and I hurled at him, and he simply did not know how to deal with us. I believe that my father has always been a sensitive man who just doesn't know how to show it, or how to talk about emotions. He probably always knew what he felt, although he never really said what he felt or wanted.

Although he is a very quiet and introverted person, my father is someone you can lean on. I think his strength was already obvious from the time I was born. My mother used to cry, fearing what would become of me, worrying if I would ever overcome being a premature infant. She was probably so scared that she couldn't function. My father was the one to visit me at the hospital, feed me my bottles, and dare to hold me in his arms. While he was not able to express emotion, he was certainly able to do the right things when needed.

It appears to me that my parents complemented one another. They divided up their roles. My mother took on all the emotional parts of worrying and crying, whereas my father was the one to depend on, lean on, and trust to do the hard work. It disturbed me that my father never expressed love, caring, or confusion. It disturbed me that he would, at times, get angry. Even when I was hospitalized, he used to demand that I eat and be angry at me for not eating, while my mother just gave up and cried. What I didn't understand then, but I do now, is that he was always doing things in my best interests, and that he really cared about me.

One thing that both of my parents agreed on was the need to hide things from other people. For my parents, showing the outside environment that everything was good, even ideal, was very important. You never wash your dirty laundry in public. Consequently, they made me hide my craziness, my sickness, and my problems for many years. In fact, they were extremely angry when I told my boyfriend (who became my husband) the whole truth about myself and my past. They were sure he would leave me as soon as he heard that I had been anorexic. I'm sure that the amount of effort they invested in encouraging me to hide the truth is inextricably connected to my constant yearning to be completely honest all the time. My need to tell the truth about myself has even caused me many problems, for example when I thought my college teachers should know about my past. After this self-disclosure, they worried about letting me study special education, fearing my craziness. But I'm getting ahead of myself, since these are recent events from the last few years, near the end of my story.

The Middle Child

I have no doubt that birth order influences the way we grow up, and the role we take on in the family. I am the second child. I believe that my position in the middle of the family affected my development. Being the middle child for me was actually being two different figures. I was the spoiled younger child for eleven years, but being two years younger, I always felt I was not quite big enough. I saw my older sister as the most beautiful and smartest person in the world, as a role model – and as my parents' dream daughter. Everything she did, she was perfect at. That's why I tore up my drawings, that's why I envied her. I wanted to be her. I tried but never succeeded in competing with her. It was a lost cause from the beginning. She was so good. She always met their expectations. There was nothing bad to say about her. She knew how to dress well, how to talk with others.

She ate the right foods and expressed the right emotions. She was always responsible, mature, compliant. I, on the other hand, went overboard in everything. I always felt different. I used to eat too much, I was not as friendly as she was, I was too emotional, I always needed to be held by my mother, I could never decide for myself.

After 11 years, I became the middle child. I loved and worried about my new baby sister. But even here, my parents allowed my older sister to care for my new baby sister, while I was considered too young, not responsible or trustworthy enough. With no responsibilities, I felt pushed away and disappointed. Only four years later, when my older sister was in the army and my parents went abroad, was I finally left to take care of my younger sister. Although at age 15 I was already anorexic, I was entrusted to take care of her for a week between hospitalizations. Again, what a double message! On the one hand, I was not to be trusted to even care for myself: I needed someone else (the hospital) to take care of me because I was a danger to myself. On the other hand, I was entrusted with taking care of my little four-year-old sister.

At the time that my parents made the decision to leave my sister in my care, I was actually in the hospital. My mother decided to take me out of the hospital. She saw that I was depressed, suffering, and had lost my joy and ability to laugh. Maybe she had become accustomed to my anorexia and was not as worried as before. My mother said that if my life was in danger, she'd rather have me die physically (of starvation) than die emotionally (lose the ability to express emotion, become depressed). My parents decided to honor my wishes to return home and discharged me. But here, once again, I find myself relating things that happened much later.

As a child, I felt my younger sister was too young to understand what was going on in my life. And I was actually afraid she might be negatively influenced by me and could develop anorexia as well. So there was a distance between us, and we didn't develop a close relationship. When she started growing older, I often found myself observing her eating habits, trying to make sure she would be different. Only recently, when she entered adolescence, did she begin to ask questions about my past. She's afraid of asking me, but when she does, I am always careful to give her the true answers and not to hide things. She is very critical of my parents' behavior toward me and unable to accept the idea that they hospitalized me. Today, she is a much more significant person in my life, because when she was a young child, I loved her but could not share things with her, and I was very preoccupied with myself. Now it is very meaningful to me that we have a close, good relationship, a real friendship.

My Grandmother

A special figure for me since birth was my grandmother – my mother's mother. She is a survivor of the Holocaust. Her parents were killed, and she was left alone at the age of 12 to raise her younger brother. She always kept all her suffering and pain from the Holocaust inside, never talking about it. Maybe this caused my mother to hide and refrain from talking about things. Only last year, when she was interviewed by the Spielberger Foundation about her experience in the Holocaust, did my grandmother begin to open up about it.

My grandmother is a very balanced person, with really remarkable self-confidence and behavior. Growing up, she symbolized for me the shift between being demanding and supportive. Despite her life history of starvation, settling for very little, fearing capture and death, and fearing the future, my grandmother was the only one who did not try to push food into my mouth. She was the only one who treated me in very direct, clear, unobscure way. She was the one to whom I ran when I argued with my parents and felt the need to run away from home. She protected me and asked my parents to leave me alone. Several times during my adolescence, she became in charge of my meals, because my parents could not cope, and with her I used to eat. What characterizes her most of all is her direct and straightfor-ward way of talking, without hiding and without apologizing for it. Therefore, she has always been the person I felt best with. You can imagine my guilty feelings when she told me that only because of me did she become ill recently. Yet sometimes I think that something about her confident manner was phony – otherwise why was she unable to share her experiences of the Holocaust? How can she behave as if nothing happened?

I often wonder why she did not become a parental figure, a model for me. Why didn't I become more like her and gain more self-confidence and have less doubt? I still don't understand how my mother came to be so different from my grandmother. It seems as if my mother acts like the Holocaust survivor, rather than my grandmother.

A Summary: What I Acquired from My Parents

As I re-read this, I am painfully aware of how critical I am toward everyone. Maybe this was one of my problems. I never liked myself, so I found deficiencies in everyone around me. Maybe only later on, when I felt the strength to accept myself as a human being who had a right to live, could I accept others and see their advantages. Therefore, I hope my parents, my sisters, and my grandparents will understand that actually seeing the bad behaviors in their lives was part of my constant search for my internal personality and my self-criticism.

If I look at the big picture today, I can say that, since my birth, I have acquired several major ideas, characteristics, and aims from my parents:

- *The need to do things perfectly,* which was the reason for my success in school, but at the same time was the reason for my anxieties and fears that I wasn't good enough and that there was no place in this world for bad people.

- *The fear (or actually, anxiety) of not doing things well,* which lowered my self-confidence and sense of trust in my own self. I never felt safe enough. I always suspected my abilities. My mother and sister were my role models, and I viewed both of them as highly admirable and extremely hard to compete with. I always felt jealous, thought I could never do things right, and tried to fit what others expected me to be.

- *An obsession with cleanliness.* Even today I sometimes have these obsessive thoughts that I'm dirty and evil, not clean. Vomiting used to be a kind of way to let the evil out of me. Rationally, I know this is not right, but I can't change these thoughts. Today I feel compelled to clean my child's room, change his clothes, etc., and these feelings even affect my sexual relations. When my husband kisses me, I turn my face away – I don't want him to be disgusted by me. Since I disgust myself, I'm afraid he'll be repulsed. Strange as it sounds, I have no problems like that with my baby. Maybe because he was inside me, he won't be disgusted. I can easily kiss him.

- *The need to hide.* As a child I always felt ashamed. I always wanted to hide. Usually people hide when they do wrong things and think they need to run away. I was always running away from myself, from others, and from the world. Now I feel as if all those years of running from people affected me in a way that makes me need to run toward people. I am not hiding anymore. To the contrary, I am opening up to everyone. I am going in the opposite direction. I feel the need to tell the truth to the people around me and to be honest with myself and others. And also I feel the strong need to express emotions, to help others, to do the right thing, to do good, etc.

All in all, my perfectionism, anxiety, and feelings of worthlessness grew stronger and stronger as I matured. As I said before, I can attribute these to the way my parents educated me, and to my mother as a role model. Just as I mentioned above, I can also relate my wish to talk openly and tell the whole truth and my urge to avoid hiding things, however bad they might be, to my rebellion against my parents' wish to conceal the things of which they were ashamed.

Yet I must admit that my being intelligent, smart, and pretty are also the results of being my parents' child. I also learned to express emotions, and I even learned to love. So, my family background is not a one-way street. I inherited good as well as bad characteristics. All I can say is that I inherited many good things that I thank them for, many problematic things that I had to struggle with, and some bad things I will never be able to get rid of and will have to learn to live with.

And What I Developed Independently

I don't think that my idea that I was bad came from my parents. I think this is something that I developed within myself. I often used to think what people could see if they looked inside me. One constant, since the time of my birth, was an idea that accompanied me intensely throughout my life: 'I am bad', 'I am not deserving', and 'If they knew who I really am, they wouldn't want me.' Right now I can say: 'Well, this is not true. I am not bad. I help others. I am a good human being. I care for people.' Yet this core idea still guides me, and sometimes even disturbs me.

As I try to look back at my past now, and to understand how I became who I was, some things are very clear. The idea of being a bad person was always there. Since I was bad, I had to be punished. So, as a young child, I remember myself doing something bad just to receive the punishment. I knew I shouldn't do those things. I knew those things should be punished, and I looked forward to being punished. I knew I deserved it. I did not reject it, and I was waiting for the punishment to come. Sure enough, the punishment always came. I was never surprised when it did.

My problems with eating were also there from the beginning. My mother tells that, as an infant, I used to vomit a lot. She always prepared extra bottles so that I could have another one after I vomited. She always feared I would not get enough to eat. She always expected me to vomit, and I always fulfilled her expectation. However, in contrast to my mother's memories, I remember myself as a child who enjoyed food. I remember exploring the refrigerator looking for something good to eat, and I remember enjoying food.

So, as can be seen, parts of who I was as I embarked on my illness were things that I inherited, parts were things that I developed myself, and many parts were things I learned merely by living in the world in which I lived, in the environment that surrounded me.

3

Between Me and Myself and My Social Relationships
Finding Creative Expression for My Loneliness

From early childhood until now, my fear of society has shadowed me. I have always felt insecure and restless around people. I always felt unequal, unaccepted, and not understood.

Even as a young child, at age 4 or 5, I remember myself fearing other people. I was very shy and always tried to stay close to my mother, to hold her hand or sit on her lap. I remember that, during celebrations in preschool, it was hard for me to actively participate, and I would not agree to leave my mother's side. I used to sit on her lap, looking at other children dancing, singing, or performing, but refusing to take part. Deep down, that hurt; I envied their freedom to behave as they pleased.

Later on, as I entered elementary school at the age of 6, it was still difficult for me to interact with other children. Throughout all the years of elementary school, until the age of 14, I didn't like being around groups of many children. So, I found one friend. Her name was the same as mine – Ayelet – and I stuck with her. We were very close friends, and we used to play together. We had fun, but I continued feeling anxiety and fear. Even when the two of us were alone, I didn't feel good. I'm not sure if she would say the same, but I remember feeling we were in a constant state of competition. I always felt like I needed to prove that I was better than she was. Of course, I never thought I was as good as her, or could be better than her, but I tried to achieve more and to compete with her for attention, success, and approval.

I never overcame this shyness. I grew up and my problems grew up with me. As a young adolescent (12 to 15 years old), this same problem continued to follow me, although it showed another face. The shyness developed into anxiety. I think they now call this behavior 'social anxiety'. Whenever I was around more than three people, I was tense, uncomfortable, anxious, and wanted to run away. I felt as if I'd been left alone in a crowd. I remember a metaphor that appeared in my mind throughout my adolescent years. In that metaphor, I could see myself as in a cage of glass. I was inside it, and the glass surrounded me. No one could hear me, and I could not hear anyone. When my anxiety was not at its peak, I could see through, but when it increased, a cloud seemed to cover the glass, and I could not see anything. I kept wondering if people knew I was there. I was among people, yet I felt so far away, different, and lonely. Naturally, the other children sensed my tension and also kept a distance.

Maybe my personal problems would not have been as severe if they had not been accompanied by social problems. I was never really an integral part of social activities or peer groups. I didn't feel good with new friends and never had many friends. I was persuaded by my parents once to attend a youth group meeting, and I felt terrible and suffered through the whole meeting. I never went again. While all the girls my age used to gather in groups, talking, laughing, joking, and sleeping over at each other's houses, I was not able to be a part of these activities. I never once spent a night at a friend's house. I was always happy for them to come stay at my house, but I felt uncertain and insecure in a strange environment. I always felt bad about the unknown. I never entered a bathroom at school, at a friend's house, or in unfamiliar public places. Even now, I will not enter the bathroom in a strange place. Even now, I hate going to hotels or being away from home.

When I reflect upon it now, I see that while growing up I kept moving between two extremes, as if I were two different people. At one extreme, afraid that I didn't deserve to be with others or that I wasn't equal to them, I would try to stay alone and to maintain my distance from other children. At the other extreme, I constantly wanted other children to seek me out, love me, accept me, and appreciate me. However, I never did anything to help other children approach me, or to even give them a signal that I was interested. I believe other children thought I was uninterested and maybe even thought of me as snobby or as despising them. I visualize myself then as calling them toward me with one hand, while simultaneously raising the other hand to stop them. As I grew, the glass cage metaphor grew stronger and stronger, appearing more often in my daydreams and fantasies.

I cannot really explain why all this happened. Years afterwards, I tried to understand what made me feel so anxious, isolated, and lonely. I think it must be related to my early problem of attachment – or actually, lack of attachment. I never felt safe and confident in my parents' presence, and maybe that prevented me from developing self-confidence, self-acceptance, and self-trust. Feeling insecure, I always believed I needed to satisfy others, and my wish to do everything 'right' aroused fears and anxiety. I did not know how to handle my wish to be perfect, so I translated it into 'not being good enough'. My insecurity also always caused me to see myself as being different from others. Therefore, I remained alone, wishing to be with others, but giving signals of being uninterested.

Looking back, I can't say exactly when this social-individual problem began. Some of the answers may be found among my early creative attempts to write and draw. As a child, I quite often sought creative outlets for my emotions and feelings. Initially, I began to draw seriously and to collect my work at around 12 years of age. My drawings changed dramatically over the years, but they were all on the same kind of parchment-like paper and mostly in black pen. When I look at them now, I am amazed to see how much effort I invested in obtaining similar pieces of paper over a period of almost eight years, from age twelve to almost twenty, including the times I was hospitalized. This uniformity was part of my perfectionism, and the parchment reflected my dramatic style – I wanted the drawings to look authentic and valuable.

My early drawings were very different from what they would become in the future. At first, my art was in color and showed some normal childhood features. Later, around age 14, my drawings would become only black and white, with an occasional splash of red. At age 15, I began invariably to depict genderless human bodies suffering and crying. Sadness and sorrow already dominated my drawings. Almost no signs of happiness remained, despite the fact that in my life I was not yet in a state of complete suffering.

A look at some of my early works from around age 12 to 13 (see illustrations 1, 2, 3) reveals that, at that stage of my childhood, I was sometimes happy, drawing themes like flowers, hands, and the sun. However, even then, that happiness was always accompanied by some elements of loneliness, or sadness, such as tears. All my drawings throughout all the years were on the same size paper (a quarter of a page) mainly using black pen, with spots of other colors.

The first drawing (illustration 1) portrayed a hand coloring a flower, most of the picture is black, with a little red and blue in the flower, and some yellow spots on the hand; the caption at the top read: *A Memory*. I was drawing something to remember for the future. The sadness is due to the fact that it belonged to the past, to the memories. The red color of the flower was gone. In the future there will be more tears than flowers. At that moment, the memory was something I wanted to cherish. It still looks naive. *Life* (illustration 2) showed the beginnings of more drama and less happiness. A child covered by a big hat, not seeing the world around, surrounded by dark clouds. Once again, most of the picture is black, with some spots of red, green, and yellow. Life at that time, at the age of 12, had already started to be dark, difficult, and fearful. In *Tear of Life* (illustration 3), there was a small house far away, a black sun, and a big tearing eye above. Tears were the main motif in my drawings. Probably, they were a main motif in my life. The sun itself was black

Illustration 1 A Memory

with very light yellow stripes. Things had already become more and more difficult and depressive for me.

During my first years in high school (ages 14 and 15), my insecurity developed into a need to constantly examine and re-examine everything I did. I was always checking, doubting, and questioning my behavior. I was never sure I was acting right. I always felt the need to check, to understand myself, to try to see if I read my internal motives accurately, and to try to become familiar with my most private emotions. I could never settle for accepting things as they were. I needed to dig and dig and find answers, and to keep asking questions about myself, my life, and the world.

Illustration 2 Life

Illustration 3 Tear of Life

At that time, I found appeal in an additional creative outlet: writing. I covered many pages, writing about my anxiety, stress, and dilemmas. I could not share my feelings with anyone; thus, I found the paper to be a good release for my thoughts, emotions, and self-examinations. Writing short stories, poetry, and stream of consciousness became my major channel of communication. I continued writing throughout my entire adolescence, throughout the time I was hospitalized. I stopped writing when I left the last hospital and have never written again, until now. When I was almost 14 years old, I was just about to start high school, which I really feared. I wrote the following:

The end of a period
that only once you have passed through it
can you find some beauty therein.
A whole new world
opens up in front of you
and it is up to you to control it,
it is up to you to locate yourself
and to find meanings, signs, hints.
Advice is being offered to you
escorting you wherever you are.
A way which lasts forever
and leaves you overwhelmed and with responsibility
for the future to come, for eternity.
Take your tools
keep all the strength hidden inside
and don't forget the expectations behind
all those and much more,
to keep you wherever you turn to
somewhere on the other side
of the door you have just opened
for you and for your environment.
Be well
take care
and keep trying.

As can be seen in this partially depressive, partially optimistic piece, everyone was telling me that I could succeed, and I was trying to tell myself that I was capable of learning and had nothing to fear. This composition clearly shows how involved I was with the issue of me standing opposite others in a controversial world. I was always trying to look at myself as I thought other people on the outside would see me, as society saw me. Constantly occupying my mind was what I meant for others, how good I was, how responsible I was. I wanted to live according to what I thought were my family's and society's expectations of me, but I felt I was failing. This poem also accentuates how I viewed my present world in contrast with some other world – the world where others lived? the world I might find in the future? my fantasy world?

Moreover, this piece demonstrates that, even before entering high school, I was already talking about myself as if I were someone else. I referred to myself in my writings in the third or second person in Hebrew – not as 'me' or 'I' but as a male-addressed 'you' or as 'he'. I think this writing style, ignoring my femininity, reflected how insecure I was even as a child. Perhaps this insecurity was an early indication of my anorexia.

As a young adolescent, I saw my life as peppered by dichotomies and multiple, contrasting qualities. The past became for me a period from which I needed to learn in order to change and have a better future. The present became ambiguous and full of question marks, doubts, and pain. This was the beginning of my looking at the present as bad. I started to develop my view of evil, of an evil drive or instinct that caused me to do bad things. I knew I was not like others. I suffered from being lonely. I believed there was a reason, a justified reason for everything. I therefore started thinking that if I was suffering, it was because I deserved it. I probably deserved it because I had done something wrong. Unable to find anything wrong in my behavior, I developed the idea that I was suffering because I was a bad person. Something inside me must have been very bad, and I had to spend my life trying to pay for that evil drive. Soon, I even interpreted wishing for something as a symbol of evilness.

Now I can see this time in my life as waving a red flag of warning, but no one else noticed the signs. Everyone thought I was special and creative. They didn't realize that I was suffering and in danger. I was already crying for help but didn't know what help to ask for, and no one heard me. I was hoping for someone to come, hold me, dry my tears, and persuade me that I was a wonderful person and should love myself and could be loved by others. But no one did. When no one understood me, I started living more and more in my fantasy world. Life was bad, so I started dreaming and living in the future. I developed this idea that, although I was an evil person in the present, some miracle would change me and I would be different. I expected myself to be a better person in the future, to be able to change my life, to be loved by others, and to love myself.

As can be seen in the next piece, I continued writing about the future as compared with the past, about my expectations for my future life, and about the significance of life. At the age of 14 I still had some hopes. I was not yet completely pessimistic. I can't tell now whether, at the time I wrote the following poem, I was actually still hopeful. Perhaps I was just trying to persuade myself that things would change in order to keep my head above the rising tide of the illness.

> *I have lots of new expectations*
> *I have a handful of wishes*
> *I have demands I didn't know before*
> *I have needs I wish to explore*
> *I want to open my eyes and see* .
> *I want to look in front of me*
> *And find a place for me to be*
> *I'd like to succeed where I once failed*
> *I'd like to have the strength to look ahead*
> *I need new skills, I need the power*
> *I need to fight and get all I desire*
> *Then...*

That drive that's in me will keep the promises
That I left behind feeling powerless
The drive will cope with all those duties
and once more look for hope and beauties.
That drive living inside me
Will soon become me and just me
New face, old meanings
No more bad, just good intentions and willingness
My evil drive will be changed and become
More realistic more optimistic
My evil drive will then be part
Of what I dream so many nights
The time has come
The hours and minutes
For new dreams and hopes to start
For confidence and trust

The drive, which later on would be embodied as the bad part of me and to which I would attribute all bad events, was already there in existence in my first year of high school. It already symbolized the problematic, bad, evil part of me. For a long time, I blamed my problems on this drive inside me that made me do things I shouldn't. This drive was the reason that I looked upon myself as a bad person, an evil personality. It may sound psychotic, but I wasn't. Inside me was also a small, innocent child wishing to grow up and do good, who struggled against the bad drive. I wanted so much to be good that I could not accept the fact that I was not. So, it was easier to put the blame on someone else who was out of my control. Around me, everyone else was good and wanted me to be good, and I felt I owed it to the others to try and be good. But my efforts failed, and I was in a constant state of fighting against the evil part within me.

I knew I was bad, but I believed I could be different. What characterized this period more than anything else was not depression or pessimism or my sense of being evil, but rather my overpowering wish to be good and to change. I did not yet want to die then. But I did already know that, if I wanted to enjoy life, I must change. Not knowing how, I kept expecting a miracle. In my dreams and fantasies, I believed it was possible. I ceaselessly waited for the future to magically solve all my past problems, like in fairy tales. I expected that suddenly the future would arrive, and I'd be different; I'd have become a better person. That future would make me feel better, and my parents' and society's expectations of me would be fulfilled. As can be seen from my writing, I invested much effort in persuading myself that it was possible for me to improve:

> *I owe you my life from the beginning*
> *So let me start the work of building*
> *I gathered all the tools for the job*
> *I think I found the best so let me go ahead*
> *I think I collected the best materials I could*
> *I will build something doing the best, as I should*
> *Something you will see as for the better not a piece of bad*
> *Something that will bring only happiness, nothing sad*
> *For a minute a tear drops down and falls*
> *But that tear is a happy tear*
> *I have no sad tears now, at all*

Once again, this piece clearly shows my ambivalent feelings. A sense of being bad and a hatred for the present, juxtaposed with an optimistic view of the future and an expectation that things would improve. Disliking my present life, I felt sad and wondered why things were so difficult. I continually gave up on my life in the present, and believed, like Scarlet O'Hara in *Gone With the Wind*, that tomorrow would be a better day. Feeling a constant debt to others, I yearned to keep my promises, not to disappoint everyone.

My poems were very similar to each other. I was very obsessed with the thoughts of good and bad, life and death, me and the world – and these motifs kept returning in a like manner in all my drawings, too. The repetition probably stemmed from my obsessiveness, but also from my deterioration and my increasing hopelessness and emotional dissatisfaction. Usually, I doubted whether I really had the skills, the strength, or the energy to cope with what life held for me. Sometimes, I felt I had the strength and could do better:

> *Now I know*
> *And soon I will show*
> *That today I have grown*
> *And tomorrow I will even more*
> *The hour that is here already*
> *Signals to come and be ready*
> *The day is about to end*
> *And tomorrow is coming ahead*
> *Tomorrow is another day*
> *A special day, a unique time.*
> *Now I know*
> *And soon all will be shown*
> *A clock that rings not to forget*
> *To learn from the past*
> *To think positively and move ahead*
> *To think of today*
> *And hope for tomorrow*
> *A star, a sun shines*
> *Tell me of order*
> *Tell me not to get close to the edge*
> *Tell me to go on, ahead*
> *Tell me there's meaning for everything in my life*
> *Tell me I have people who care for me*
> *Tell me I have a life.*
> *Today I know*
> *And tomorrow I'll show*
> *And from tomorrow all of you will see*
> *My promise to thee*

Not only did I look forward to a better future when I wrote this, but I also wanted everyone to realize that I'd changed and become a better person. I am not sure who 'everyone' was. My parents? Friends? Teachers? Whoever they were, I already knew that I was different from them. Knowing that I was not like other people around me, I was already warning myself not to go past the barrier or break the limit, to stay inside the frame. I guess I was afraid of the outcome if I showed everyone how much I deviated from the norm.

Although I did look ahead toward the future, my fears had increased. I was so busy fearing, running away, and expecting things to change. I didn't understand that, actually, the fears did not come from the outside world but rather from within. I didn't understand that there was nowhere to run. As Tammie used to tell me much later, if we run away from our fears, those fears chase us, and they certainly did then. I was hunted and haunted by those fears. Lots of fears.

I often wonder whether someone professional, a therapist, would have been able to recognize all the signs then – my doubts, my feeling of being bad, my fears of the future, my fantasies and expectations. If so, could my sickness have been prevented? Could my problems have been solved without evolving to the extent they did? Sometimes I think that I was only a typical frightened adolescent who was dramatic, sensitive, and so scared that normal problems grew into a tremendous grotesque illness. Could it have been prevented?

I guess I will always question that and never know the answer. For me, the future could not be prevented. I was traveling at such a speed that I could not be stopped. I had to keep going on, and I could not stop myself. I expected the worst and, sure enough, it came. I was looking for a better future, but I had to wait such a long while before I reached it. I was inside quicksand, fearing I would sink, hoping to drown, yet still looking for someone to miraculously save me. But miracles don't happen in normal life.

Before my sickness, I hated the present and looked toward the future. Later on, when I was sick, I could no longer see the future. I was sunk deep into the ugly present. Or maybe it was the fact that I had lost my future – any dreams, fantasies, hopes, or expectations I'd had – that made me become sick. I don't know what was the cause and what was the effect, but either way, my future disappeared.

4

The Stage is Set
From Healthy Child to Anorexic

Re-reading all of what I've written so far, it becomes obvious to me that my sickness did not arise out of nowhere. The hints were there since I was born. The problems could be found in all areas of my life. I don't know if anyone who knew me could predict that I was going to develop such a distressing illness. But I always knew. I didn't know what to call it or what form it would take, but I knew something bad was on the way. I could sense the internal signs. I could hear the cries of warning.

I did not have social ties, which are so important during the teenage years. Looking at society's role – if social relationships are a predictor of one's adjustment – the clues were already apparent. Alone and lonely, I did not feel a part of society. Being among others only highlighted my differentiation.

I believe we develop our self-image by the way we are viewed by others. We develop self-confidence when others trust us and accept us. We start to believe in ourselves when others give us feelings of worth. We learn to know ourselves from the way our personality is reflected in the mirror that society holds up in front of us. We are reflected in the mirror of society. Unfortunately, there was no mirror held up in front of me, so I could see nothing. My parents did not help me see myself in the right way, and I had no social relationships to help me with that either. I was always blind to my own reflection, never knowing what was real in relation to myself.

Looking at my family's part, I understand that instead of feeling protected by them and learning coping skills from them, I felt alone, criticized, neglected, and isolated. In the mirror they held up, I did not feel I fulfilled their expectations. I never received what I wanted from them. They did not help me cope with my insecurity. They never tried to understand what was really disturbing me or to help me express my distress. I felt they preferred me not to share my emotions and fears. I felt it was easier for them to ignore what I was experiencing. They preferred to close their eyes to what was really starting to develop.

And when I did sometimes succeed in seeing my own reflection in my family's and society's mirror, what I saw was so different from what others saw. Others thought me a sensitive, pretty, smart little girl. Can you believe that they even thought I was a good girl? Others never saw the sorrow, the pain, the fact that something was so very wrong. No one could tell. No one else saw. So, how could I be expected – me, a little girl – to see, to understand, and to change all alone? I wanted to get out of it, but I wasn't sure what 'it' was, or where and how to get out. And I couldn't cope alone, without help.

Within myself, I felt doubts, conflict, a lack of self-assurance, and even evil. So, actually, there was no where I could feel good, and no person who could help me find myself and my place in the world. With that, the stage was set for developing depression, suicidal behavior, and anorexia.

5
Flowing with the River
Learning to Act Anorexic

So, I was starting to flow with the river, and I had no strength to stop it. Just as stones are carried along by the intense force of deep waters, I felt myself to be helplessly and completely taken over by what was happening. I felt unable to change, stop, or take responsibility for the flow of events and experiences surrounding my development. That flow was mighty, deep, and rapid – much stronger than me. I helplessly rushed onward with the current, unable to change the direction of the tide, heading right for illness.

When I think about how my anorexia developed, I can see that its foundations – in the form of all my problematic thoughts and emotions – were already present during elementary school. But gradually, during my adolescent years, they became more focused and deeper, and eventually established themselves as problematic disorders. The doubts that always accompanied me, as an integral part of my life, turned into real pain. The process of suffering, of checking and rechecking who I was and what was inside me, became harsh and constant. I was incessantly unsure of who I was, what I was doing, and whether it was right or wrong.

This nonstop process of digging deep into my body and soul was not helpful, to say the least. My shyness and uneasiness turned into anxiety, fear, and self-destructiveness. I was trying to hide from the world and wished to remain unseen. The fears, the perfectionism, and the wish to behave well and look good made me dread growing up and resist the normal process of maturing and developing. Growing up meant the unknown, something out of control, and I didn't like losing control. I did not want my body to control me. I feared emotions and sensations, so I did not want to experience my growing sexuality. I searched for some internal cause for my problems, thinking there was something bad inside me. For me, a child was a symbol of innocence; so, naturally, drives, sexuality, and growing up became symbols for evil. I wanted to be good; therefore, I wanted to stay young. I was afraid that growing up would expose me to internal needs and drives I might not be able to control. Even today, I resent things that I cannot control, and I always try to be in control. Thus, I started to reject food, and slowly even to starve. At first, in order to stop my growing up. Later on, to gain a sense of control over myself. That was a predestined route toward becoming anorexic.

If I had to select a specific date for when my normal insecure behavior turned into a sickness, I would pick my 14th birthday. It was during the Passover holiday. I had expected my two best friends to initiate a birthday celebration for me. I waited, but they didn't even remember to congratulate me. I was very offended. I blamed myself for being a dull, uninteresting person who was too fat and not charming or attractive enough, which was why nobody really cared about me. Reproaching myself, I thought that if I were a prettier, smarter, or a better person, everything would probably be different.

It was after this birthday disappointment that the desire to change my situation, change my social status, and make people want me intensified. It was clear to me that the best way to achieve the social success I wanted would be to change the way I looked. As a child, I had always been chided for eating too many unhealthy and unnecessary foods. I enjoyed eating junk food and sweets and didn't really care for healthy, good food. At 5 feet 6 inches tall and 123 pounds, I wasn't fat, but I believed that if I lost those extra 4 or 5 pounds, I would look better without them. Always obsessed with what others thought of me, I decided that the Passover school vacation was a good time to make the change. I was occupied by thoughts of how surprised everyone would be when I returned to school thinner after the holiday. I used to imagine the way they would look at me, appreciate me, and like me. I was also occupied by thoughts of showing everybody what I was capable of accomplishing and how good I could look. I used to think that, once all this happened, they would all regret the way they had treated me, and would like to be my friends.

I was surprised to see how easy it was for me to go on a diet. I was always a person who tried to live up to the challenges I set for myself. I started dieting without any hesitation. The first few pounds disappeared easily. Giving up junk food didn't make me feel deprived. I had no difficulty giving up sweets, and even fasting felt worthwhile, although it wasn't easy. The pride of my success made me feel very happy, and for me, feeling happy and successful, after all those years of feeling worthless, was the most important part in the process of dieting. However, reaching one goal usually meant that I immediately wanted to start working on the next one. I could never settle for what I already had. Each time I attained a goal, it was a signal for me that I could do it, and that it wasn't as difficult as I used to think. Consequently, I continued to diet, establishing new goal after goal. By finding concrete goals that I could achieve, dieting also became something that made me happy. In addition, when I stopped eating junk food, my family was pleased. Suddenly, I felt my parents' unmistakable approval, and I didn't have to doubt whether my behavior was a good or a bad one. Seeing that my focus on dieting made me put my sorrow and anxiety aside for a while, and that my change had pleased my parents, I went on dieting even after the holiday ended. Actually, I learned several things from this first stage of dieting:

1. It was very easy to be on a diet, once I decided to do it.

2. After a while, it became easy and less painful.

3. Dieting was a shelter from stress and anxiety.

4. Dieting gave me satisfaction, happiness, and goals to look forward to, and I was not used to having those emotions.

5. Dieting gave me the feeling that I was not weak, but rather a strong, capable person.

Thus, dieting became a symbol for all the good things I wanted. Why should I stop? By the summer vacation, three months later, I felt I was succeeding very well in losing weight. Dieting and losing weight had become very easy for me. I was also feeling much happier than before. Hence, I continued dieting, or more accurately I should say that I began to starve myself. Although at first it had been difficult to fast, later on I didn't suffer. To the contrary, strange as it may sound, I would gain a certain satisfaction from the pain itself, from the sensation of starvation. I think that, partly, this stemmed from the idea that I was alive and could actually feel things – even bad feelings – and partly it was a sense of strength in overcoming and controlling my body.

By that time, dieting had slowly begun to become the central target of my life, the happy part of it, the part in which I was succeeding. I felt resolute, powerful, and proud. Success gave me the energy to continue, but each time to a greater extreme. During summer vacation, I decreased my food intake considerably. I thought my parents didn't know. They seemed to be happy with me and didn't seem to suspect anything. At least, they didn't say anything. I have no idea whether they noticed my starvation or not. At the time, at 14 years of age, I wrote in my diary:

I was lying on my bed without a motion
Thinking about how to find a solution
Looking for a color between white and black
Expecting an answer to help me with that.
Then I was sitting near the window
Just watching the wind blow
Looking for the beginning up to the end.
Now I am standing there
Behind the door
Hating to be in and afraid to be out,
Looking at the floor.
Don't know where I should be
I am here and you are there, and who is me?
Feeling alone in that horrible war

Trying to succeed, overcoming failure
And still hoping, still wishing to find someone who
Is as good to others as he is to himself
Who looks around him, behind him, in front of him
And even next to him.
I want to be with him, to learn from him,
And to share my life with him;
Then the answer will come, the real justice;
Then the right color will be found
And my real place in the world in general
And especially in life.

At this age, my drawings continued on the same kind of small parchment-like paper I'd begun using more than two years earlier.

Illustration 4 Luck

The drawings were made in black pen, and only a few very bright colors could be noticed. As can be seen in illustration 4, I drew a boy with his head deep inside the ground, and another child walking away, who can be viewed only from the back. I drew only figures with an unclear gender, with their faces hidden. No girls and no sexuality. Were these cues regarding my wish to hide away and cover things? Was I trying to hint something to my parents, who acted as if they were not aware of what was going on? I called this drawing *Luck*. I think it was my cynical way of saying: 'No luck. I have no luck in life. I'm stuck in this suffocating, dismal place, and I'm alone, even abandoned.'

The summer vacation ended, and I entered high school. I was in a very competitive class. My grades were excellent, but being good was never enough for me. Even being the best was not good enough. I always felt I could do better and should do better. Yet I was always tense about success – never sure whether I could cope with it. Anxiety, stress, and insecurity were much more familiar companions. They always stayed with me, and I knew they would never leave me. Thus, instead of thinking about my studies and fearing them, it was natural for me to occupy myself with dieting. Losing weight was a place I felt secure in – my ability to control myself and to overcome all temptation – and it kept me busy. In fact, soon I was obsessed.

My writings show that the issues of life and death were always in my mind, even then. I remember that by the age of 14 I was already very interested in death. I already knew then what I wanted my grave to look like. I would imagine a big gravestone and often picture my grave and funeral. I contemplated cemeteries often, although I wasn't permitted to go to one. I did not fear dying. To the contrary, I was curious, I wanted to die. I wondered what it was like. I decided to give my body to science. As I became sicker, I started to talk more about death. I saw it as a solution to my problems. I also became obsessive about death. I was fascinated by death and I wanted to feel it. Even today, I think of death very openly, often, and without any fear. I just wish for my husband to be buried near me when the time comes.

My massive involvement with death began when my cousin died. She was ten years older than me, and I wasn't at all close to her. But I admired her when she became sick with cancer and had to cope with all the pain. She became a model for me – of suffering, pain, and coping. She used to be the one to cheer everyone up around her. Her death was a turning point for me. Death became part of my life. I thought of death, I wrote about death. I was not allowed to attend my cousin's funeral, but I was very interested in it. Upon my cousin's death, the family published a book about her. I could never let this book out of my sight. I slept with it and took it everywhere. I was not depressed. I saw death as a solution for problems, as a way to escape all distress. I was expecting it. I wanted to learn firsthand what it meant.

At that time, right before my 15th birthday, according to other people, I was really thin. (I myself never felt thin enough.) I was 5 feet 6 inches tall and I already weighed about 101 pounds (after I lost lots of weight during Passover and the summer vacation). I was obsessed, anxious, and occupied with death.

It was my ninth grade teacher who first noticed the dramatic change in me. She invited my parents to school for a talk, but they never came. I think they were afraid to hear the truth so they preferred to act as if they knew nothing. It might also be a part of their tendency to hide the 'dirty laundry' from others. The teacher was probably worried about me, so when my parents did not come to her, she came to visit our home. I suppose the teacher had decided she should warn my parents about my condition. She confronted them and insisted that they listen to her, saying that she thought I was an anorexic. This teacher was the first one to call my illness by its real name and to recommend urgent therapy. However, my parents did not want to see the truth, and they did not believe her. They thought she was just too anxious, and that they knew me better. They said I had always had problems with food, and had always vomited. They said I was sensitive to food, and that losing weight was a normal behavior for a child my age.

At that point, I was already an expert at being anorexic. I was already well experienced at hiding and throwing food away, forcing myself to vomit, and deceiving my parents about what and when I ate. At first, I tried to hide things from my parents. I used to furtively take food that my parents expected me to eat and hide it in bags, which I would later take outside and discard in the garbage bin. Then I started forcing myself to vomit several times a day. I became obsessed with vomiting. I soon found it very easy and effortless, and, once again, I felt good about controlling myself. Here was another aim I had achieved – another challenge I had conquered – and another success of mind over body. I guess it was a lost cause from the start, because I interpreted these deprivations and self-mutilations as achievements and successes that made me happy. As my condition worsened, instead of understanding the damage I was perpetrating, and trying to change things, I viewed everything as a new goal or challenge that offered a chance of feeling good about myself. It was very exciting for me to constantly set up new goals and targets and to actually achieve them, one by one. I loved this feeling of accomplishment. It gave me strength. So, there I was, losing more and more weight, vomiting, deceiving and hiding things from my parents – and feeling satisfied. Yet my satisfaction was never complete, because, whatever I did, I always felt I had another mountain to climb. I always wanted something more.

As can be seen, my drawing (illustration 5) at age 15 already pointed to anorexia. I drew a female, but she looked male. There were no signs of her gender. As in almost all of my other drawings, her face was covered, this time by what seems to be the weight of the world. Aptly, I entitled the picture *Burden of Life*. She was very thin, and I focused much more on the details of the body than I had in the past, portraying a more lifelike figure, rather than the earlier caricatures. Yet, at the same time, there were fewer details in this picture. My world had become emptier of details other than myself and my diet. There were also fewer colors – mainly black. There was a hint of another female figure looking down from above. From heaven? A

Illustration 5 Burden of Life

hint of somebody who still cared? I don't know. Although her eye is closed, the large face is the only one so far unhidden. I am not sure what I thought then, but I know I was always occupied with seeing the truth and being hidden from the world. I was trying to convey some unknown message.

Thus, the constant feeling of success, self-control, and accomplishment, along with the desire to look good and thus gain friends, were all factors in losing weight. Yet, I would say that my fears of growing up comprised a major component. I had always feared growing up. It felt like I was battling a kind of fight about who would be stronger – me or my body. Not wanting my breasts to grow, I would bind my breasts with a long scarf or a very tight shirt like they used to bind girls' feet in China, hoping to prevent them from developing. I wanted to hide my maturing bosom and would avoid wearing a bra.

When I got my period, I suffered from very heavy cramps, which I wished would stop. A period was something dirty, an ugly symbol of pain, but also a sign of growing up and becoming a woman. Thus, losing weight seemed to be a successful way to prevent both distressing cramps and growing up. And, sure enough, I succeeded in that as well!

I developed a comprehensive plan. How much I had to eat and how much I should get rid of. How long I allotted myself to stay in the bathroom in order to throw up and rid myself of all the food I'd eaten. How much energy I had to exert to lose weight and how long I should exercise. I used to run around my room in order to lose more weight. I was preoccupied and obsessed with all these aspects of my program. I enjoyed the sense of control I felt I had. Losing weight kept me busy from the minute I opened my eyes in the morning until I closed them at night.

Wanting my parents to stay in the dark as to what was going on, I spent much time in my room, with a closed door. This probably made it easier for my parents to ignore what was going on. They didn't seem to notice, or at least acted as if they were unaware of my activities. Surprisingly enough, despite my incessant preoccupation with my body, I could still learn and succeed in school, which helped perpetuate the pretense. One day, I did not lock the bathroom door, and my mother came in while I was undressing. She was shocked. She said she could see my bones. But still, she did nothing to force me out of this situation. I saw my bones as well, but, unlike her, I was gladdened by the sight. I wanted to feel my bones. I saw this as proof of my success, and I was happy that I no longer had that ugly fat on me. Strange as it sounds, I don't remember this time (the beginning of anorexia) as a difficult period, as suffering. On the contrary, I felt mostly power, success, and control – a sense of joy in suffering.

It is interesting how vividly I remember the feeling of success from losing weight, whereas I cannot recall the physical pain of starvation at all. Yet I used to long for those moments where I could eat. I loved and enjoyed eating. Food was something to enjoy, but I believed I didn't deserve joys or pleasures. I developed the belief that I deserved to suffer. This belief of being undeserving has always followed me. Even today, I sometimes ask myself: Do I really deserve all this goodness, joy, and pleasure that I have today? What good did I do to earn it?

So anorexia was the outcome of my personal problems that were always there and my social problems that led me to start dieting, as well as my relationships with my family, which prevented them from stopping me, confronting me with what was happening, and demanding that I do something about it. The fact that my parents kept ignoring the truth merely helped me continue quietly with what I was doing. When they finally allowed themselves to admit there was a problem, it was too late to stop me. My father thought I should be hospitalized long before my mother did. They used to argue a lot, but he would always acquiesce to her. My mother was too optimistic. She believed in me and was afraid of harming me if she were to insist on hospitalization. This, together with her tendency to hide things, helped her to ignore the situation. If I had to paint my parents, I would portray my mother in very bright colors and my father in dark ones. Living between the white of my mother and the black of my father, I was always in the gray. I never knew what or who was right.

At that time, at school, my classmates started calling me 'half a human being'. The teachers were worried, and the school nurse insisted on weighing me every week. However, the school was helpless to do anything more, due to my parents' lack of cooperation. In contrast to my peers', teachers', and nurse's intentions, I enjoyed and was reinforced by their attentions. I liked being called half a human being. It served my purposes; I felt I was on the right track. I was unaware of the danger of my situation. I liked achieving my aims and being the center of attention. Thus, I faced a divided reaction from others. On the one hand were concerned classmates, teachers, and nurses, and on the other hand were my parents, who denied my problems and didn't know how to cope with me. Throughout my high school years, my parents continued to avoid the real problem, moving from one extreme of shouting at me and forcing me to eat, to another extreme of being indifferent and letting me do what I wanted. I felt they were weak, so I could continue doing what I wished. I gradually increased my vomiting, began using laxative medications, and continued to hide and discard the food served to me.

Getting all these mixed messages from those around me was very tiring. I felt helpless and exhausted. I could not find answers within. As I've said earlier, my image in the mirror had always confused me (and still does). The one that I saw then differed greatly from that seen by others. I could never understand why other people didn't see me the way I saw myself. It was like having two, completely different figures. I was so disconcerted by that incongruent. I could never

Illustration 6 The Bird of the Soul

figure out who was the real me. This gap became stronger and deeper as the sickness evolved.

My drawings from that time lay bare the suffering I was experiencing. One drawing (illustration 6) was called *The Bird of the Soul.* Usually, while relating to the bird of the soul, one talks about wishes, expectancies, or fantasies. For me, the bird was black, frightening, scary. I hated what was inside me, I wanted to get rid of it. It looked like a raven rather than a nice, small songbird. I think it's very meaningful that, instead of drawing the bird inside the person, I drew the person inside the bird. The bird was in control, while the person was being controlled. The second drawing from that period (illustration 7) depicted a view from behind of a group of faceless people. It is

Illustration 7 The Outcry for a Solution

called *The Outcry for a Solution*. In a gesture of prayer, these people were looking for some help from above.

When I was a little over 15 years old, I started hearing voices. I thought I was psychotic. Not far away from our home there was a psychiatric hospital, where I was hospitalized long after. As children, we always feared this place. Children used to point to it and say that it was a place for crazy people. Crazy people for me were those who heard strange voices, saw unreal figures, and said stupid things. So, as I started hearing voices, I knew I was crazy. In treatment, Tammie asked me about those voices. I explained to her that I used to hear an internal voice telling me that I was evil, that I had to improve, that things weren't going right. Afraid of what was happening to me by then and especially afraid that I was a bad person, I found a great

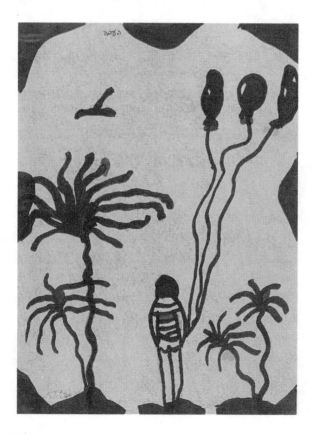

Illustration 8 The Past

solution in hearing voices. I could now say that I was not at fault – it was the voices I heard who told me to do what I did. I understand now that, in line with my perfectionist nature, it was easier to blame someone else rather than myself. It helped me then to imagine that it was not me, but rather some internal force that caused me to act the way I did. I always used to relate myself, to write about myself, in the third person. Now, it was even easier to talk about someone inside myself, to relate to that voice as another, strange, separate entity. This figure was always male. I am not sure whether those voices were a way to separate myself from my problems, trying to cling to life and save my sanity. Maybe my fears and insecurities about my own sexuality

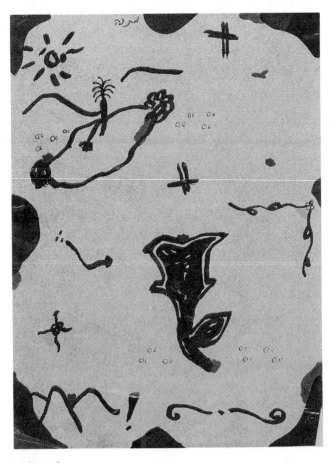

Illustration 9 The Gift

made it easier to relate to the male person inside me. Maybe it was just a denial of my incessantly deteriorating condition, or it could have merely been, as Tammie suggested later on, my regular thinking that I heard.

I was suffering, but I resisted help. I knew I was in a bad state, but I was angry and resentful. I couldn't understand why people were interfering with what was going on between me and myself. It was not as if I were harming my environment. So why was it other people's business if I harmed myself? Didn't I have the freedom to make decisions about my own life?

My drawings at that time were all black and depressive. In one, *The Past*, a girl holding balloons can be seen from behind (illustration 8). But, unlike the colorful balloons children usually play with, my balloons were black. So were the trees, the sky, and the flying bird. There was no happiness, no fun, no promise in my world. In a second drawing (illustration 9), *The Gift*, I was expecting a sun, a tree, some joy. However, the gift I received was black, small, insufficient, and unhappy. I am not sure whether it was a flower or a dying butterfly, but it was surely something meant to be alive and beautiful but marred and aberrant. What kind of gifts could I have expected? There was no joy in my future. Nothing to look forward to.

6

Receiving the Diagnosis
'Yes, I Am an Anorexic'
My First Experience in a Psychiatric Hospital

When I was a little over 15 years old and had already been anorexic for almost two years, I still thought I could fool the whole world. Yet, it came to a point where my parents could no longer close their eyes to my state. The high school demanded that my parents act, and this time insisted that my parents take me to therapy as a condition for my continued school attendance. Reluctantly, facing no alternative, wishing that I continue my studies, my parents agreed to take me to therapy. I don't even remember that therapist or what we did together – probably nothing meaningful. I went for two sessions and refused to continue.

For me, being anorexic was feeling power, my forces. Proving to myself that I was strong and could control myself. Often, teachers and nurses warned me that I could die, but I laughed at them. I did not want to die. I only wanted to test my abilities. Touching death, playing with it, without actually dying. Feeling my strength and power to move between the two worlds of life and death. And, perhaps (which is what others would probably say), getting the attention I'd always sought. I felt vigorous and empowered by my dieting and would not relinquish that sense of power without a fight.

My parents first became active at initiating my treatment when I was less than 16 years old. It was then that they first began to insist that I needed help. I was taken to the first hospital in a series of many more that I would get to know. That first treatment was conducted on an out-patient basis in the psychiatric department of a general hospital. I attended group therapy meetings for girls with eating disorders. The group included girls with anorexia and bulimia. Before each session, we had to step on a scale, weigh ourselves, and show the psychiatrist the note where our weight was written down. Then the group discussion started.

At first I was very passive. I was there and listened, but I didn't take part in the conversation. I hated those meetings and didn't want to be there. I felt I did not really belong to that group of girls, some of whom were in-patients. I knew that my weight-related behavior was not right, but I didn't want to be changed, so I didn't cooperate. The group lasted for an entire year until some of the girls were hospitalized and some were referred to individual treatment. The group became a real support system, but the support was not what the therapists expected. It was not support for fighting our problems or for trying to change ourselves and our behaviors. To the contrary, the group became an arena for competition as to who could lose more weight and who could best deceive the therapists. Between ourselves, we avoided issues such as how old we were, how tall we were, or what our lives looked like before the sickness. All we cared about was who succeeded in weighing the least. Hence, instead of providing support for overcoming our problems, this group supported us in overcoming the therapists' pressure to change. I remember coming to the group and listening to one girl who had tried to commit suicide. After this attempt, she was hospitalized. I envied her. I felt she had succeeded more than I. She got more attention, she was stronger, she was braver than I was. I wanted to be like her. This was my first actual thought of really trying to harm myself.

I learned from the other girls in the group about different kinds of medication I could use, both for emptying myself, and for trying to commit suicide. I learned that I could mix different kinds of pills together in order to kill myself. I started using all sorts of drugs but none worked well, or maybe, unconsciously, I didn't take enough because I did not really want to die. So, I continued to vomit, to hide food, and to starve.

My eating patterns were very rigid. I was obsessed with my eating and ate almost nothing, with the same regimen every day. It was like some kind of a ritual ceremony. When I was forced to eat bread, I used to cut it very thin so it was almost transparent. When my parents were angry, and I had to compensate them by eating something, I would eat three little beans. When my parents were relaxed and didn't interfere, I didn't eat. I used to eat a yogurt in the morning, eat several (3–5) beans for lunch, and drink water. When forced to eat a fruit, I used to cut it and peel the skin in a way that left no flesh. I used to drink water but colored it so my parents would think I was drinking something good.

Even though I was not active in that group, those other girls from that hospital, like the other girls from other hospitals I would meet later on, became my real significant friends, my support group. They were like me, and they could understand me, my behavior, and my world – unlike everyone else. Much of my writings and thinking, later on in the future, were directed toward them and were about them. They were my most significant others for a long time.

During all that time, I was still waiting for someone to take charge and stop me, to put limits to my behavior, to prevent me from continuing on that course. But no one did, and I continued flowing with the river. I was too weak to take charge and try to stop myself. I was playing a game between life and death.

My parents, peers, and therapists often told me what I should do, how I should change, how I had to take charge of my life. But I was the biggest expert at telling myself what I needed to do, although I never seemed able to do what was necessary. This is also reflected in my writing – giving myself orders, trying to warn myself, and instructing myself to avoid and reject others' suggestions:

I tried to tell her
but she didn't listen.
It came out exactly like it came in.
I tried to send her some hints
but she never understood.
I told her to stop
and she went on and on...
I told her not to give up
but she already turned.
I told her to stop
but she continued on her way.
I asked her 'Why?'
and she never answered.
I never existed for her
I knew where she was going
I knew I had tried
I only wanted to help
but it was as if she felt betrayed...
I understood her future
I wanted her to know as well

It was as if someone else, inside of me, some internal voice, was expecting what would come about later on, and wanted to stop me from continuing down this one-way dead-end street, with no way out. But I could not listen. I ignored my own voice. I blocked myself out. I closed my eyes, shut my ears, and refused to listen to myself. I had the feeling of an inner battle between me and myself, between relating to myself as 'I' or as 'she' and later on as 'he'.

No one ever saw my writings. Everyone – my parents, my friends, and even my therapists – knew I was writing. But everyone looked at them as the immature behavior of a young girl. No one ever thought that my writings could reflect what I was experiencing or could help in getting through to me. I could not tell them what I felt, I did not know how to express my feelings. So my only outlet for expression was in my writings. I wrote and wrote, covering tens, hundreds, thousands of sheets with my pen. I feared the future. I was already aware of the fact I was in danger, and I wrote:

> *I tried to prevent what*
> *might have happened*
> *but I did not succeed.*
> *I had good intentions*
> *but they never had a chance.*
> *She never even looked*
> *and never turned her head*
> *never let out any voice*
> *never showed any signs.*
> *She just went on and on*
> *but when she remembers*
> *and might look back*
> *it will already be too far.*
> *The gate will already be locked*
> *the opportunity will be lost*
> *it will be too late.*

That was the warning I always heard from others: 'When you finally understand how difficult your situation is, it will already be too late.' Too late, too late, too late, too late. Was it already too late? In a drawing (illustration 10) from that time, *Only Me*, I drew a girl hiding her face, trying to cover herself. She was thin, had no signs of sexuality, and wanted to hide herself from the world. She wanted the world to disappear. Nothing was happy around her. Only thin black trees. Whatever it was she was feeling and experiencing, no one on the outside could know, although one can sense her gloom and loneliness.

In all my writings, there were signs that I was going the wrong way. That something terrible might happen. The knowledge that I should stop and avoid it, or the hope that someone would come and help me. I felt lost but still had some hope. I felt I could not stop on my own – and waited for someone to stop me. The only productive things I did during those years was writing.

Illustration 10 Only Me

You know what is going to happen
but still you do nothing
you know it is about to come
but you do not move from where you are
you want to warn, to hint
to talk, but you know your actions are
in vain
you understand what he wants
you listen to his words
you even hear what he doesn't want to say
you read his thoughts
together with his emotions
you know of his intentions
you know exactly what is going on

and also are sure of what will be
you know because actually
he is just you, like you
that drive inside of him
was seared inside of you
but you know that only he himself
will understand it by the end
and this knowing will be in vain
since he never changes his aims
you feel so hurt
you could prevent it
you feel so sad
nothing can actually be changed
as if you are in it again
everything comes back, returns,
you dream that soon it will be over
you wish he would understand and look over
at your hope
just hope for him and for you
since he is actually you, just you
the drive that is seared inside of him
was seared inside of you, too

As I wrote this, I still held some hope of being able to stop and change, but at the same time wished to continue on my path. I was caught between two mighty forces, and, inevitably, I found myself going with the flow, flowing with the river.

Time passed, and group therapy was a failure. I didn't want to stay in the group, so I left. It was obvious that something must be done with me. My parents thought that individual therapy might be better than group meetings. So, a short time after my 16th birthday, I started individual therapy with a therapist from the same hospital. This treatment did not help either. I did not cooperate. The therapist did not understand me and concentrated mainly on trying to make me eat. I think I must have been a challenge to that department, because soon the head of the department started treating me, thinking that he might succeed where others had failed.

I have no deep emotions about that treatment, which suggests to me that it wasn't really significant. Everything seemed static during that treatment. I remember the eating disorder and the continuous fighting at home, but not anything important in therapy. The sessions were dull and boring, focusing on what I was feeling, going on and on. Again and again, unsuccessfully trying to bring me to talk about myself. I think the first person to start feeling depressed was my therapist, from that psychiatrist department. I soon followed him. The treatment, the unsuccessful treatment, pushed me to depression, to the big black hole. I could no longer see any gray or white, or bright things. I was in a terrible dark hole, and my therapist was in a black empty hole, too. There was no way to get out. The only good thing about this was that my future therapists would have something more to treat. A new diagnosis – my depression.

I was obsessed with emptiness, nothingness, and depression. I turned this emptiness, these black holes that I felt, into my own philosophy of life. The philosophy of emptiness and big holes. I remember how, when I started therapy with Tammie and told her about the big black holes, she said that she was not familiar with my vocabulary and asked me to explain what these meant to me. That was when I understood that the big empty hole had actually turned into a big empty whole, coloring everything black to me. This black hole of nothing, that had turned into a black whole of everything, started later on (in therapy with Tammie) to change colors and size, and then it disappeared, but that was long after.

So, I was in treatment that did not help, I continued being anorexic, and then, I became really sick. Not sick in my mind but sick in my body. I felt something in my breast. The same breast that I did not want to let grow, and, when it did, something was wrong with it. I didn't tell my parents, as I never shared things with them. I went alone for a physical examination, and, as it turned out, I was right. I had a lump and was referred for a surgical biopsy. I was very scared. Now, I really had something to be frightened about, and I was really expecting death, but it scared me instead of making me happy. This was not the kind of death I had envisioned.

When my parents found out, they forbade me from having the operation. I can't understand why. Was it their way of putting things under the rug, believing that if you don't talk about something, it doesn't exist? Anyhow, I felt old enough and independent enough to ignore them, and I decided to have the biopsy. I was a scared young adolescent who made a huge decision alone and did it feeling lonely. Angry at my parents, I did not want them to come with me to the hospital or to visit me. I decided that if I were to be alone in this, I would do everything alone. And if I died, then they would feel sorry and regret everything.

I can't say that I didn't care about life, because I remember it was important for me to go through with all the examinations and the surgery to remove the lump. I guess it was a sign that I didn't completely want to die. When someone really wants to die, she succeeds. I guess I didn't want to die – I wanted to suffer and to punish myself. When I was told that the lump was not malignant, I was very happy, and, for the first time in a long while, I felt relaxed. I knew that my time had not yet come. Even now, it is hard for me to think about myself as a young girl going through all of that alone. I would not want my children to be alone in such a situation, and it is hard for even me to understand how I could have been brave and determined enough to do that all by myself.

Of course, I didn't tell my therapist about any of these events, so she could offer no support during that difficult ordeal. In fact, therapy did nothing to help. Therapy would go on and on, in different settings and with different therapists, for the next several years. Each year pushed me deeper into the big hole I was in. Every year I continued to feel there was no way out. They gave me lots of diagnoses, strange labels for stigmatic clinical situations, and I started to fit them. If they called me anorexic, I could be the best anorexic on earth. I could use more medications and more sophisticated attempts to gradually kill myself in more sophisticated ways. They saw me as sick, powerless, and depressed. No one tried to turn to my positive side, to look for my strengths, or to try to persuade me that I possessed some good things inside myself as well as the bad. I was treated as a diagnosis, not as a human being. No one cared about my hobbies, my joys, my writings, my expectations. They only cared about my sick behavior. If I was obsessed with food and fears, they were obsessed with trying to look, dig, and find all the monsters in my past that made me anorexic. It was like a game we played as to who was more obsessed. When I got tired of it all, I just gave up. I tried to fit into what they thought of me. If they wanted a sick person, that's what they got. I really became sick.

Thus, in a pattern that would repeat itself over the next years, my out-patient treatment in the first hospital by different therapists terminated. It had achieved nothing. We had all become more depressed, until they all finally understood the message and left me alone. I came out of it knowing nothing at all about how to get better, but I knew much more about how to deceive, hide, vomit, and lose weight than I knew before I started. I even added some important information to my repertoire: I had learned immensely about all sorts of different medications and ways to commit suicide, and discovered new and innovative ways to resist others' attempts to make me gain weight.

7

My First Hospitalization (Second Hospital)

Or: Who is Stronger – The Illness or Me?

My first hospitalization was at the age of 17 and a half. I was in the middle of the last year of high school. It was just before graduating. All my peers were in the process of preparing for being drafted into their mandatory military service after graduation. It was clear that my physical condition would prevent me from serving like the others. My parents, together with my previous therapist, thought that I should be hospitalized for a short while. They believed that being hospitalized would help me solve my problems quickly in order to gain weight and join the army like my peers. They believed that it would help me to be under others' supervision, with regular meals served to me and the company of people who expected me to eat. Thus, I encountered my second hospital, a different one. In order to prevent a psychiatric entry on my personal records, which could impair my future, my previous therapist suggested that I be hospitalized in the children's department of a general hospital, not in a psychiatric one.

Consequently, I ended up hospitalized for six weeks in the children's department, where I received treatment by psychiatrists from the psychiatric department. Yet, I was allowed to go home whenever necessary in order to take my matriculation examinations at school. It was like a game we all played. No one wanted to say I had a psychiatric problem, so all of us (my parents, teachers, therapists, and myself) acted as if I had a medical problem needing treatment. This ensured that, when I left the hospital each time to go to school, no one could question where I was.

Being hospitalized in the children's department was actually fun. I was among the oldest of the children there. I remember helping the children and the parents in the hospital. I tried to keep the little kids busy and happy. I felt as if I were in a summer camp. I used to go, play with the children, have fun with them. Actually, I enjoyed their company much more than I used to enjoy my own peers' company. Being the oldest made me feel equal, worthy, good. I felt no competition. I did not feel inferior, and I felt people (or actually, the children) really liked me. There, I really felt I could act myself. It was an integral part of me to want to take care of others and to help people. Even then, I knew that whatever I would be doing in the future must involve working with others who needed help. It was natural for me, later on, to learn special education. On the other hand, I never could help myself. I was constantly neglecting myself and my own needs.

In that hospitalization, I did not live in reality. It was like a game. I woke up in the morning and went to school to take my examinations. Afterwards, when it was time for my classmates to go home or to hang around with peers, I went back to the hospital. It was like being in a shelter, where no one could harm me. I felt protected. But actually, no one really interfered in my life, and I could continue going on my own self-endangering way.

As for my physical condition, nothing changed during those weeks. The food in the hospital was terrible. The mere smell of food in a public place made me sick, so it was ridiculous to even contemplate the idea that, in that place, with that horrible food, I would change and start gaining weight. As you can imagine, I lost more weight. This time, I had become so skinny that even I stopped seeing myself as too fat. But my obsession with losing weight was no longer related to how I really looked or how much I weighed. My condition didn't improve, and even worsened. I started feeling bored and saw no reason to stay there any longer. I hated doctors and didn't believe they could help. Against all advice, I took my things and left the hospital. Failure number two. But was it my failure? The doctors' failure? The triumph of anorexia? I could no longer be sure who was winning and who was losing. I didn't know anymore what I wanted and what needed to be done.

I was promised that the hospitalization would be short. I was always good at talking and at persuading others. So, I succeeded in convincing my parents and my therapists that there was no reason for me to stay at that hospital. I believe they also wanted to get rid of me. I was a strange creature, and they had no idea how to help me. So, I was allowed to leave the hospital and go back home. They recommended that I continue individual therapy as an out-patient of that department. I agreed, mainly because I thought it was the only way out.

I came back home. My condition regressed more and more. Physically, I lost more weight and it became very difficult for me to eat. I was weak, and I did almost nothing. Emotionally, I was very depressed. I started wishing to die. For the first time, it was not a game anymore. I stopped feeling I was controlling things. The good feeling of losing weight had changed. I was really suffering. I was no longer attaining any good feelings out of my situation. I tried to avoid thinking about myself. I spent my time dreaming, sometimes hallucinating.

Again, the only productive thing I did during that time was write. My writings reflected my condition and started becoming obscure. Even I myself cannot definitely explain what I meant. I started using more and more third person and the masculine while writing about myself. Mainly I debated with others my right to die. I was occupied with death and dying. Death started looking like the best solution. I used to think of my death. See my funeral. Long for the time when I would no longer be alive. In my writings then, I referred to myself as someone else – he – but he was actually me. Was that a clue to the fact that I was trying to stop my sexual urges? Did I fear them? Or was it just craziness? I have no idea.

And he lies there
And he is happy and sad
He has to decide between life and death
The doctor says: 'I have to do what I was assigned to
You might be able to make your family happy too'
'Doctor, I'm a lost cause
Leave me, turn your face away'
'My patient, you should never give up life
You have to stay with us and survive'
The patient then replies: 'I will live there, in heaven
I am on a path of no return'
'Dear patient, what if you only try to survive?
The miracle might bring you back to life'
And he answers: 'I live and will live on medication
Look at my family, they lost their patience'
'Oh, patient, think again, maybe you are wrong
Try and give life a chance, you might feel strong'
'Oh, doctor, look, there is no law that exists
The solution to my problem is not in your hands
You know I rebel, reject, and resist…'

My helplessness and depressed feelings were intensified by the fact that none of my therapies had helped me. I had the feeling that now my therapist at this second hospital had also given up and had no idea how to treat me. I said I wanted to stop coming to sessions, and, consequently, that treatment, like its predecessors, was terminated. I stopped this last therapy without sorrow, feeling that it wasn't helpful anyhow. Yet I began asking myself: If all those professionals gave up on me, wasn't it a sign that I was in a very bad state? Was I a lost cause?

I persuaded my parents that the hospital was not for me, and they suggested taking me to a psychologist in a private clinic while I lived at home. I liked this idea more than the thought of being hospitalized again, so I agreed to cooperate. I returned to live at home and started a new therapy process.

8

Is There Anyone Who Can Help Me?

As I started private therapy, I agreed to the psychologist's terms that while under her treatment I would receive regular psychiatric check-ups in a hospital (a different one). I had no choice, if I wanted to avoid hospitalization. I guess that this condition that she established stemmed not from her fear for my well-being, but rather from her desire to cover her tracks while treating someone whose life was at risk. This private treatment was, until Tammie, the longest therapy I ever had. She treated me for several years, and from time to time used to meet my parents as well. Most of the sessions focused on my family background. Believe me, my family background could occupy many therapies. Any therapist would appreciate finding such a rich history of suffering and pain: the family's Holocaust survivors, history of avoiding problematic areas, and need to present themselves as a nice, good family and to hide their problems from others.

At that time, I was very ambivalent toward my parents. In a way, I wanted to continue fighting with them. I thought they couldn't understand me, and would never understand me. I felt they had deserted me. I wanted them to worry, to understand that they didn't treat me well. On the other hand, I wanted them to accept me and love me. I wanted their protection and their help. Emotionally, I was still a child. I desperately wanted to be able to see my parents as godlike figures, as role models, as the ones who knew best, as the ultimate authority. I was badly disappointed by the fact I could not see them that way. I was angry at them for not fulfilling my wish. I was angry at myself, for not being able to accept them as I thought I should. Thus, I was confused and lonely, feeling like I was walking aimlessly in the darkness.

I don't think anyone can be helped by someone they don't like. And I didn't like my therapist. I hated those sessions. We talked about things, but I had this sensation of eating food that had already been chewed, or walking in very thick mud. My therapist was incessantly busy digging and digging, and that was so tedious. Maybe she was a good therapist – it's hard for me to tell. But she certainly was not a creative one, in that she never seemed to try to change the style or the way in which we worked. It was so predictable and so useless! How could I be helped if I was bored – with myself, my stories, and my therapist? How could I change if I felt sick of just talking about it all over and over again?

During the previous years, I often suffered from being sad, anxious, and lonely as accompaniments to my weight loss. Now, I could add clinical depression to my original problems. Yes, I could not hide that fact: Now that my condition had deteriorated, my depression had become severe. I think the sessions were probably very depressive for my therapist as well. If I were a therapist, I would like to treat people by teaching them how to be happy and find delight, not how to become heavily involved with their sickness and sorrow. Also, I believe that some humor or interesting discussion might have helped at times. I know it is probably my depression that made me see the world in black, and made me criticize my therapist. I don't want to sound as if I blame my therapist for my condition. She certainly didn't cause my problems. I am also sure that she had the best intentions. However, I feel that she did not help me find a way out. We got nowhere. I saw no way out of the blackness.

During that time, while I lived at home, my mother felt she had to do something to take care of my eating problems. At first, she tried to prepare my meals and watch me eat them, but we always ended up arguing about what I was eating. So, my grandmother, the one to whom I feel very close up to this day, offered to take responsibility for my meals. I did not want to eat. However, my grandmother was the only person for whom I unambivalently and deeply cared. I didn't want her to worry or to become sick. I agreed to go to her house for some meals, which also enabled me to avoid having to listen to my mother's begging and urging me to eat. My grandmother made me eat a little. She never argued or forced me to eat. She would serve me only the kinds of food I was willing to try (vegetables, cheese, diet foods). I began to eat only over at her house. We didn't argue, and I was ready to cooperate, feeling that this was better than being forced to eat everything. I didn't gain weight, and that satisfied me. But at that time, I stopped losing weight. I was not as stressed as before. Maybe that was a good starting point.

9

Meeting the Big Black Hole

My First Attempt to Commit Suicide (Third Hospital)

I was 18 years old. I had graduated high school with academic success. I have no idea how I succeeded in taking all those matriculation examinations. I was depressed, anxious, and very, very thin. I was weak, tired, and felt cold even in the middle of the summer. Still, preparing for those exams had been something productive to occupy me over the last years. Now school was over, and the tests were over. Because my condition had not improved after that brief hospitalization, I was persuaded to postpone my army enlistment. I didn't want to go, but I also didn't like the feeling of being different. All my classmates were starting their army service. There I was, the only one who could not be drafted. I stayed at home, doing nothing all day long, every day, day after day. I had no more schoolwork to occupy me, no friends, no fun, and no real aims to look forward to.

Suddenly, even more than before, my whole world seemed to be black and empty, and I felt so lost in the dark. I started feeling as if someone had emptied everything out that had been inside me. The world around me also seemed to be empty and vague. It was then that I started really seeing how my life was full of black holes. Some of those holes were ones I sought while trying to commit suicide. Some were those I felt I was thrown into by my therapists (all of them) by their digging, digging, and searching for nonexistent answers.

Experiencing my first attempt to commit suicide was my first real meeting with that black hole that had previously only been a metaphor, and which continued to accompany me for a long while in the future. It happened at the end of that summer after graduation. I had been going to the hospital for weekly check-ups for the four months since my discharge from the second hospital, and, because my condition showed no improvement, the psychiatrists wanted to hospitalize me again. The psychiatrists already understood that I might try to commit suicide. (Like so many professionals' predictions for me, this one came true as well, in another self-fulfilling prophecy.) But this time, I refused to agree to be hospitalized. I was already 18 years old; therefore, I had the legal right to decide for myself, and they did not coerce me. So I stayed at home until that first suicide attempt. Did I really want to die? Was I doing it because they were expecting me to? Did I want to prove that I was not being helped? Was it a call for help? Did I want to test my own strength, to see how far I could go? Was it a game? I'm not sure that I took suicide seriously. I don't believe that I considered all those explanations at the time.

I was at home alone during the days, and I started to collect all kinds of pills. Many of them. One morning, as my mother left home to go to work, I swallowed all of the pills at once. I don't think I thought of death. Surrounded by the image of my classmates who were living their lives as usual, serving their country in the army as all 18-year-olds are expected to do in Israel, and comparing them to myself, I felt overwhelmingly alone, lonely, and helpless. I wanted time out. I wanted to be unseen. To see another world. To take time out and come back.

I took all those pills together. After a few minutes, I felt dizzy. I went to lie down in bed. And then, I had a real black hole. I lost contact with time. I had no idea where I was or what was going on. I don't remember anything about that day. As I was told later on, my mother came back home, and she thought I was asleep. For a long time, she didn't do anything. Was that, again, her way of avoiding unpleasant things? After a while she heard noises and entered the room.

It was when I started vomiting that my mother first realized that something was wrong. She took me to the shower. She turned on the water and washed me. She took me back to bed and I fell asleep and remember nothing. Then, my father came home and saw me, and immediately decided to take me to the hospital. Next thing I knew, I was opening my eyes in a hospital bed. That black hole I experienced was the total depression, the time-out from the world, being unseen, not feeling, not knowing who I was, where I was, and what would happen. I guess this time I really scared everyone. My parents decided that I could no longer be responsible for myself and that they had to take charge. They forced me to be hospitalized.

I was still dizzy, and I felt very dry. I was receiving liquids intravenously and was not forced to eat. I didn't want my parents to come and see me there. My psychiatric assessment at the time granted me with my third diagnosis: suicidal personality with depressive patterns. As I came back to my senses and stopped feeling so dizzy, I wrote this poem, referring to myself as 'you' and to everyone around me in the normal world as 'they' – my peers, my parents, my therapists, the doctors:

> *You are descending while they are climbing up*
> *You are dreaming while they are doing, acting*
> *You are failing and they earn their success*
> *You keep losing and they are gaining and showing a happy face*
> *Something is going on in your world, not in theirs*
> *While your world is dying, theirs is blooming once again*
> *You only know, while they understand*
> *While you only look, they can look and see*
> *While you only think, they can see, view, and think*
> *You are only you, while they have become another*
> *While it is easy for them, you keep suffering and suffering*
> *It is so deep for you, and they are on the surface*
> *You are being called, but only they can answer*
> *It looks like the end, they are at the beginning*
> *Since you have changed, they have not*
> *You are sad, they are happy*

The smile left your face, and moved to their faces
You lost words, and they found them
Since that's what you are, and they are others

Well, I was 18 years old and already confronting my third hospital. Like the first two, this third one was also a general hospital. Apparently, my parents still didn't think things were so bad. They refused to admit or to accept the fact that I was trying to commit suicide. Ignoring what they had been told by the hospital staff, my parents said, or believed, that it was only an accident. Instead of seeing the dangers of the present, they were still more concerned with avoiding the damage to my future that records of a psychiatric hospitalization could render.

Once again, as I was moved to this third hospital, no one understood me. As always, I turned to find solace in my writing. Writing was a comfort. There, I could be myself and let out all my fears and expectations. I was very dramatic, seeing the world as completely dichotomous, probably like most adolescents but to a greater extreme. When I read some of my writings now, I smile, but it was so serious for me then. I took myself very seriously:

> Young child – I miss you. Your sudden smile, the pain that is not familiar to you, the constant attempt to run and compete with yourself. The nonstop look for things you cannot afford. The wish to be an absolute organism in the universe, who controls but is not under control. You walk through life and life is dangerous for you. You can't even see how dangerous it is. The vacuum that is being created under your obscure figure, is the only one that never leaves you. When did you lose your eyes, your ears? When did you stop tasting and smelling and noticing every little change around? When did you stop being smart and intelligent? Where did this anger come from? This heightening fear? This rebellion against life? The demand for meaning and answers? It seems, kid, that these questions will occupy your mind and your soul throughout all your life. There is no one but you who bears this kind of burden of questions and solutions. You will awaken for the day as if the light is so obscure. During the day you will be

escorted by your insides, drives, and internal world, by yourself. As night comes, you feel as if you still haven't done enough. You feel you have to look at your life and learn from it, and stop it. You occupied yourself with checking and rechecking yourself again and again. Enough. Choose, child, a flower. A flower without a thorn that could cut your face. Choose, child, a flower. A flower with a fragrance. And a fragrance that also has a taste. And a taste that brings relaxation and a smile to your face, that can erase the sadness in your eyes. Take a flower, kid. It's yours. From childhood to adulthood. Take it and hold it tightly. Always here, in the spring of your life. Be successful, stay well. Amen!

As can be seen, I was, again, talking to myself as 'you' (in the Hebrew masculine). I was trying to give myself instructions to change. I already realized that I had wasted my life, and that I shouldn't continue along that same path. I wanted things to be better. I wanted to smile, I wanted to enjoy flowers. I wanted to – but I couldn't. I could find no joy, fun, or happiness in my life.

My feelings at that time, right after my attempt to commit suicide, could also be demonstrated in my drawing (illustration 11) called *To Fly Far Away*. I wanted to soar away from there, to cease existing as I had. To stop the pain, to stop the sorrow. To fly away to a better place. I am not sure if I meant to die, or to try to find a better world with better understanding. Certainly I wished to be elsewhere, not in my regular environment. As can be seen, I was depressed, but it was a different kind of depression. I saw my world as bad, black, and lacking meaning. But I believed another world existed. A better one, where flowers, hope, and love could be found. I did not really want to die. I wanted to live better. I was just not sure where or how I could find this better world, and, sometimes, death seemed to be the solution.

After I came back to my senses and was no longer groggy, I refused to eat. As a result, I was fed through a nasal tube and gained a few pounds. At that time, I was 5 feet 6 inches tall and weighed about 97 pounds, which was 26 pounds less than I was before I started dieting, but a little more than I had been several weeks earlier. I was fed nasally

Illustration 11 To Fly Far Away

for a few days before I was moved to food. It was then that the hospital staff started calculating my caloric intake and selecting high-calorie foods for my diet. That frightened me more than any previous diet regimen. As they calculated calories and used a food scale, so did I, but for the opposite purpose. Now, I had something new to work on and become obsessed with: calories. No one related to my mind or my soul. Food was only an external symptom, but it became the goal of those therapists.

My parents were not allowed to visit me. It took my parents two weeks before they asked for special permission to come and see me. I stayed in that psychosomatic department of the general hospital for four months. During that stay, I only visited home twice for a few hours each time. Each time I went home, I collected pills, knives, sharp objects, etc. to damage myself, so they decided to stop my home visits. I was not permitted to go home for weekends – something that other patients were permitted to do.

The staff were very nice to me. The supervisor, teachers, and nurses were all trying to be understanding and to express affection, but I was scared of the world. I wanted to change but was afraid of changing. I wanted to let people in, felt I needed them, but couldn't. So, I built up a high wall, and no one could get through. Everyone saw me as a troublemaker, as someone who was fighting the world and trying to make things difficult. Actually, I was a frightened little child, but no one saw the scared little girl in me. All they saw was the manipulative teenager who tricked them, was very dangerous, and could damage the environment and herself. All the while, I was longing for attention, warmth, love, and caring. I needed protection. I felt more and more lonely. The worse my feelings became, the more I thought it was a sign that I was really bad and that no one would ever be able to help me. I blamed everyone for not giving me love and affection, but the truth is that I don't think I let anyone love me. I was not in a position to accept love. I did not think I was worthy of love. So, there I was, wanting hugs and empathy but receiving pain-inducing needles and injections, and remaining unable to enjoy or connect to the warmth the staff expressed toward me.

Illustration 12, of faces, is called *The Shadows*. Everyone seemed like a shadow to me – meaning that they weren't real people to me. I did not really feel them or relate to them. I was not aware of their particular personalities or emotions. They all seemed the same. Each one was just another face nearby, treating me, looking for me, ordering me around.

I can still recall from those days my fear of the long dark corridors. I was constantly being taken for another check-up, another examination. I remember the endless corridor, with many suffering people on its sides, shouting and yawning, people crying for help, and me walking between nurses, powerless, as I was led to more and more examinations. Neverending examinations.

Illustration 12 The Shadows

The department itself did not look like a hospital. We were allowed to wear our own clothes, not hospital gowns, and the beds were regular furniture, suiting teenagers. But the doors were locked, and one had to buzz to open them. There was a painted line on the floor near the head of the department's rooms, and we were not allowed to step over it. We were three to four girls in a room. Those who were in better condition could go out and spend an hour alone. But I was not allowed to.

There was a fixed daily routine. School during the morning, group session and therapy session during the afternoon, and family meetings once or twice a week. I spent most of the time in the lobby or in my room. The other girls were very different from me. There I first met girls from a very low socioeconomic status. I also met anorexic boys, and some with other psychosomatic problems. I got along with the other girls but never got close to them. We had nothing in common to talk about. They were different from me. There I met a religious girl, and I was shocked. One of my misconceptions was that these kinds of things cannot happen among people who believe in God. Religious people, to me, seemed to be good people. God loves them, so how could they become sick? Only later did I realize that there are no rules. Sickness is not a punishment and therefore can affect good or bad people.

There was a kind of competition between the girls. Everyone wanted the others to recover, but for herself to stay thin and sick. The worst thing was knowing that I was always being looked at. I was never left alone, always under supervision. Everything I did was being watched. It was hard to hide, vomit, or get rid of food. Still, I succeeded in not gaining weight. I had no time for myself. And I was concentrating too much on myself and my sickness. Living from one minute to the next.

I was afraid that someone would take my pen and papers away. So, I used to hide them, and draw and write secretly. In illustration 13, I drew a tree, with people as a part of it. There are three people in it, or around it. They look like monsters – very thin monsters. That's how we all looked. I called this drawing *The Tree of Life*, but it actually looked like the tree of death.

I wrote a lot during that hospitalization. I was 18, hated my world, and was looking for answers. This next piece of writing depicts the split I felt inside me. 'Me', 'her', and 'you' all referred to myself. Inside, I was split between the bad and good parts of me, between the part that wanted to die and the one that wanted to live. I was not sure who I was, and I was so confused:

Illustration 13 The Tree of Life

I do not know why
She just doesn't understand
Why is she going in the opposite direction from me?
Her steps pull mine
And I move backward
The end is so far
The light
I don't know why
She just doesn't understand
But I am failing with her
I don't succeed as well
I have tried again and again, nothing changes

She doesn't give up
I don't know why she just doesn't understand
Not always hearing
Never listening
Never understanding
Sometimes doesn't see
Never looking
Not always wanting
I never know what she means
Not always forward
Never to continue
It is so hard to know, understand, listen, see, hear, look
When you are alone
You need power which is like yours
A bird that can understand your soul
It is impossible like that – just to understand,
To push me in the right direction
Not toward the darkness – toward the light
I am just being pushed and I wish to know where to
I don't know why she doesn't understand
And I
For better and for worse
Follow her

I secretly listened to the staff discussions, and I heard the way they diagnosed me. They said I was very sick. I agreed, and I think this gave me legitimacy to be really sick. I decided that if I was so sick, then I could give up. I could act like a crazy person, I could be schizophrenic, and I wouldn't have to try to cope any longer.

I think the doctors were confused by me, as can be seen by the various diagnoses I received. One thought me to be mainly anorexic, another saw me as depressive personality, the third one thought I was a borderline personality, and the fourth was impressed mainly by my self-destructiveness and suicidal behavior. The fifth was sure I was schizophrenic. If they could not agree on who I was, how could I, a young girl, confused and powerless, know who I was? I think they often tried things out on me, without really knowing what to do or what would be effective, and without success. Every failure for me was a new sign of how bad I was, how hopeless my condition was. Meanwhile, it was like I was doing an internship in psychiatry. I learned the different diagnoses. I learned how each of them should behave, and, believe me, I was intelligent. And I had also grown up believing that others knew who I was better than I ever would. So, when I was called borderline, I could be one. And if they said I was schizophrenic, I was really sure that diagnosis fit me.

There in that hospital I was really sick. I felt sick, I acted sick, and, as I felt I could lose no more weight, because there was nothing more to lose, I became more and more confused. Perhaps the medication contributed to my feeling of being remote and light-headed because I was receiving so much. I started being mentally sick. I produced fears, delusions, illusions, and self-destructive behavior. I say 'produced', but I don't think I understood that I was doing it on purpose. This is my understanding now of what happened then: in order to stay sick and fit my diagnoses, in order to give the doctors the symptoms they were seeking, I reported and showed them. When they asked if I heard voices, I heard them. I really believed I was psychotic until Tammie redefined those voices and helped me understand that it's completely normal for people to talk to themselves. What I'd been hearing was myself; it was my own voice and thoughts. There was nobody I could talk to, so I talked with myself. It took me many years to understand that the self-talk I experienced was not only very normal but could even be an important coping skill rather than a symptom of illness.

Hearing voices was a very simple solution to the split I felt inside. Okay, so I was hearing voices. It was easier, in a way, to throw the blame for my predicament onto others. Then it wouldn't be my re-sponsibility; it would be the fault of those voices who told me to do things. When people were angry at me for not eating, for not socializ-ing, for trying to kill myself, I could say: 'Hey, it's not my fault. I was told to do that. I have to listen. I have to obey!' The 'he' to which I would refer, when writing about my drives and urges, grew bigger and took on the form of voices ordering me around. No therapist then questioned whether this presence was or was not real. Nobody suggested that perhaps there was no one inside of me but myself. That, actually, I was debating with myself, having self-dialogues. That it was not psychosis, but rather a kind of self-talk. On the other hand, maybe these dialogues were a big factor that helped me get through my ordeal. The fact that I was debating meant that I was not completely sure I wanted to die. I was not giving up but, rather, was still arguing with myself. But no one offered these alternative ideas to me at the time, and I myself thought about it differently only much later in my sessions with Tammie.

With the voices I heard, I also started visualizing. I saw images. Those images were not clear, but they were surrounding me, ordering me to be sick, and thus reinforcing my wish to behave as a sick person, the way they expected me to. I think I was afraid to admit that I didn't want to recover and that I wanted to die; therefore, I constructed those voices and images to tell me to die. My fears magnified. All of the fears that I would suffer from later on were beginning to grow: fear of the dark, fear of being alone, fear of harming others, fear of others looking at me, fears and more fears...

I saw myself as being in the middle of an intersection. Fearing to take one direction, because it might be the very wrong one. Hesitating between the different roads, and, therefore, staying stuck in the middle where it was so dangerous, with all the cars coming toward me at rapid speed. What characterized this period for me the most was darkness, confusion, doubt, and terror.

With the fears, I started developing stomach aches. They didn't know what was wrong with me and wanted to refer me for what was to be my first-ever gynecological examination. I was frightened by the idea that some doctor would check my female organs. I was ashamed and scared, and I resisted the referral. They insisted that I go to the gynecological department. I refused and cried. There was no one to accompany me, reassure me, help me understand that it would not be painful and that no harm could come of an examination. After I refused to be examined, the hospital announced that they could no longer be responsible for me. Due to my lack of cooperation, there was nothing more they could do for me. I was told that this hospital was not a psychiatric one but a general one, and that my condition was too problematic to continue being treated there. They thought my condition necessitated a closed unit in a psychiatric hospital.

The regional child psychiatrist saw me then, and she told my parents that they must take me immediately to be admitted into a psychiatric hospital. If not, I would be hospitalized by force, under legal order. It was Friday. I wanted to spend the weekend at home, but I was not allowed. My parents, concerned that I might be taken by force, rushed me up to the regional psychiatric hospital. They did not try to question or rebel this decision. They just did it. It was not easy for them. My mother cried. But they did it.

10

In the Cuckoo's Nest

Behind Closed Doors

In all the movies and books, 18 years of age is a time for romance, love, joy, parties, and laughs. I was a little more than 18 and was spending my life in hospitals. This time, in the fourth hospital, I'd ended up in a place for really crazy people. I understood at the time that my parents were being compelled to admit me, under the threat of hospitalization by force, by law, without asking my consent. But I was still very angry. No one asked me what I wanted, what I needed, where I thought I should be. I was sent over there like a package being delivered.

All the way to the hospital we were quiet. No one could really digest the situation. Much later, in family therapy with Tammie, we talked about what it had been like for my parents to put me in that place, how they had felt. It was terrible for them as well. They were ashamed. They finally understood what a terrible state I was in, and they were helpless. At the time, we never talked about it. They just complied and said nothing. And I kept quiet, as always.

Not only was I excluded from the decision making, but I was also kept in the dark as to what was going on and what to expect. I never got any explanation about where I was going and what it would be like there. Having never been to a psychiatric hospital before, all I knew was gleaned from frightening movies and stories. And it ended up that the hospital they sent me to was one of the worst. A facility for chronic cases. Among professionals, it is considered one of the most difficult institutions. It seems that no one had taken the time to consider what an impact that experience would have on me or to plan my hospitalization in a more appropriate hospital that took my own needs and best interests into account.

The first image I recall is when we stopped the car at the entrance. A man was being constrained. I was shocked, and so were my parents. My feelings upon arrival are evident in my drawing (illustration 14) called *A Dog's Life*. I drew a black dog under a tree, with a couple bones nearby, and labeled it 'Me'. I felt like a dog, I was being treated like a dog, and I saw nothing good waiting for me in the future.

As Tammie and I were writing this part of the book today, my mother called. She was minding my son, Or, while we were working. I asked

Illustration 14 A Dog's Life

her how Or, then four months of age, was doing. My mother replied that she and Or were having a conversation. I asked her to mimic to me how he was expressing himself to her. Then I found myself imploring her to let him say anything and everything he wanted. I told her: 'Just remember that he's only four months old and can't really speak yet.' I asked my mother not to let Or bottle anything up inside: 'Let him pour his chest out.' I guess this is important for me because, during the most significant period in my life, throughout my entire childhood and adolescence, no one talked to me about what I really felt, and I said nothing. Emotions, fears, doubts, and pain were all left inside untouched, and this is something I do not want my child to experience. I wonder if in my new family, we will be able to talk about everything, share fears and maybe tears, and hug each other and lean on each other in a way that fits each of us, our true internal needs. Wouldn't it be easier for all of us that way? I think of how very painful my admission to the psychiatric hospital was for me and for my parents, but no one admitted it aloud – and again I felt alone and lonely in my experience. When I asked my mother over the phone today to let Or say anything he wants so he won't keep things inside, she asked me if this sentence belongs to me or to Tammie. I don't know. I know I can talk things out now. I have learned to, and I want my son to be able to do it. When I started being able to talk, I could stop writing. But that was much later.

Getting back to that terrible psychiatric hospital, my parents admitted me and left me there. I was left all alone in a room, and I was really scared. I remember the small room, with one bed and a small barred window that faced the nurses' room. I really felt like I was in the cuckoo's nest. Here I was, a teenager, and the youngest patient in that hospital was about ten years older than I was. Most of the people there were my parents' and grandparents' age.

Typically, the more difficult my situation was, the more I used to draw and write. I want to share here two drawings from that time: *Isolation* and *The End*. In *Isolation* (illustration 15), I saw myself in a closed room, sitting between two huge, frightening faces. Only through a thick barred window could I see the world, with its sunny day and free, flying bird. The world inside that room was a different one, horrible and closing in on me. In the next drawing, *The End* (illustration 16), I wanted to stop the suffering. ('Stop the suffering' is written on the hand.) Far away, inside the fingers, there were flowers, a little house, girls, a tearing eye, and the sun. But all those were distant. Close by there was only pain.

If I had to be assessed after that hospitalization, probably the best diagnosis could be post-traumatic stress disorder. My experience

Illustration 15 Isolation

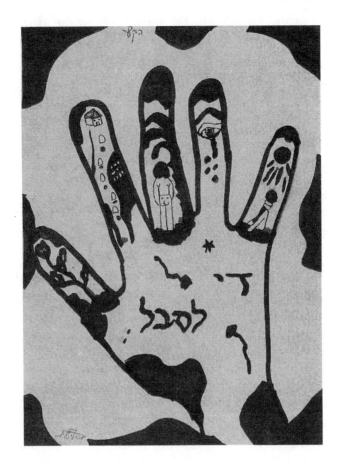

Illustration 16 The End

there was truly traumatic. Nevertheless, as it turned out, that very traumatic experience was the only thing that woke me up and made me find myself again. I realized that I had to prove to everyone that I wasn't sick. I had to show that I didn't belong there. I, therefore, collected my greatest strengths and skills together. For the first time ever, I tried to fight for myself. And for the first time after a long period, I started acting normally again.

When I first arrived, the admitting psychiatrist read the report I'd brought with me. He told me that he'd been asked to place me in a closed, locked unit. He hesitated for a while and then said that he could not do that to me. He said that he was sure I did not belong in such a unit. He also said that he felt terrible about the idea of placing me in a closed unit. Instead, he decided to place me in an intensive care unit adjacent to the nurses, where I could always be watched. I didn't even feel grateful. I was so shocked that I felt nothing, indifferent. Everything seemed to me like a nightmare. I was waiting to wake up.

I stayed at that hospital for a month. The most terrible month in my life. The longest month I've ever experienced. The atmosphere there was passive, depressive, and lifeless. There was no communication between the people. Everyone was busy with themselves, and, if they did talk, it was only to themselves. I could only communicate with my parents and the nurses.

When I compared my situation to all those people's, I didn't know if I should laugh or cry. They all moved very slowly, probably stoned out on the psychiatric medication. They didn't talk clearly. Most of them never knew another home. They were chronic patients who were afraid to leave the hospital. They felt safe and protected there. Compared to them, I was very vibrant, very healthy, and very happy.

This hospital was the second which replied to Tammie's request for information. They diagnosed me as a borderline personality with a secondary diagnosis of depression. I wasn't really treated at that hospital. They held an occasional individual discussion with me. They tried to find out more about my condition. Sometimes, I participated in a group discussion in which I was not active. That was the only hospital where I felt and acted healthy. I wasn't ready to play the game anymore. There, I stopped comparing myself to normal people in a normal environment. When I compared myself with those very sick patients, who live inside closed doors, for the first time in my life, I felt healthy. I continued taking the medication they prescribed, and I started eating because I wanted out. I became really healthy and normal there. The psychiatrist, as well, thought I was too normal to stay there, and recommended that I leave the hospital. For once, we all had the same evaluation of my condition.

Happier than ever, I left the hospital. Although coming back home had been my fantasy during that long month, I found myself terrified of returning home to be among normal people. In fact, I only stayed home for two weeks. The dream had been a happy one while I was out of my house. Once I came home, it wasn't that easy. I discovered that I was afraid of being at home. At home, I started therapy with a new therapist. This time, it was the head of the psychiatric youth department in a different, fifth hospital. She tried to help me talk about my problems and understand their sources. We were digging deep into my past and my problems. It was like falling from the sky. After a period of being happy, feeling strong and healthy, playing the normal person in the previous hospital, I felt sick again. Always talking about being sick, sick, sick.

Through therapy, she persuaded me to be hospitalized in her hospital's youth department, believing that my situation was bad and I needed intensive help to improve. I felt I no longer knew what was good for me or what was true. I let her convince me. My parents were not sure that hospitalization was the solution, but they didn't argue. They let things happen without really interfering.

Being among normal people, being with my family, and needing to cope with a normal life scared me. Comparing myself now with normal people again made me feel sick once more. For the first time, I was happy to be considered a psychiatric patient. I was happy to agree to the hospitalization.

II

Fifth Hospital
Will I Ever Be Normal?

I cannot remember the first few days at this fifth hospital. It's as if someone erased that first week from my memory.

In previous hospitalizations, my parents were prohibited from staying with me during the first weeks. According to what they told me later, this time they were asked to accompany me and remain with me 24 hours a day for the first days to avoid the shock of being hospitalized in a psychiatric hospital. It was the longest of my hospitalizations – I stayed there for eight months.

In the department, there were adolescents aged 12 to 22, boys and girls together. What characterized those kids most of all was the feeling of being miserable and the atmosphere of sickness. No one could see a light at the end of the tunnel. It had the feeling of some chronic, static disease. Nothing changing, nothing optimistic – as if we were asked to accept the idea of being sick and learn to live with it. I felt again that I'd received a license to be sick and needed to behave like a sick person. If I felt healthy in the previous hospital, I certainly felt sick in this one. There was no outside world, no healthy society – we were completely disconnected from the real world. Inside was sickness and just sickness. Maybe this was the reason why I stayed there for such a long time. Eight months is almost a whole year. A year that, outside, could be full of joy, happiness, youthful experiences, excitement. But in that place, there was nothing. The time came when I no longer believed that I would ever be able to live outside the hospital, without treatment, without being taking care of.

The staff were angry at me for not socializing with the other youths. They blamed me for isolating myself and for keeping myself busy with my writing. They used to take away my papers and pen. I hid little pieces of paper, and I would write at night, in the dark, and hide my work under the mattress:

I asked her: 'Why?'
She said: 'Just accept it, it's from heaven'
That is God's will
And I closed my eyes.
I asked Him: 'Why?'
And He said to me: 'Stop it. This is destiny.
This is the choice that remains'
And I closed my eyes again
I asked them: 'Why?'
And they told me: 'Stop. It's luck'
'It's how you were born'
And all by themselves my eyes shut
I asked myself why
And I could not answer
I tried to open my eyes
I opened one halfway, the other was afraid to look
One tear, and even two
Streamed down on my face
Nice pleasant views
And in front of them the difficult, the bad one, the terrifying
One…and two
I closed my eyes and reopened them
I thought something would change
But the change was only in me
I knew! I'm not sure I understood
I heard. I'm not sure I listened.
I sensed. I'm not sure I felt.
But I tried.
Big confusion, tremendous chaos
Inside and outside
A sharp, tearing pain, never stopping

One eye shuts. The other tries
A tear or two to express what was left
And then the two are shut
I moved a little
I wanted to make sure
That I could see, really see
Yes. The eye.

And I wrote and wrote. It was my only relief. The paper understood me, never criticized me, never blamed me:

Fear of life…anxiety…fear of death…I was just a lonely person. In my heart, my broken heart. With pain, and sorrow. Listen to the voice, the voice which is quiet now, a far away memory…a dream, half hoping, half looking for promises…

I met death. He was wearing a strange face.

He came suddenly, without warning. He came and asked me to join him…I knew death was the loss of power…maybe nothing was left of me…I know that if I cried I'd be left behind…I had to run, I had no strength…

I've always been turned from a friend into an enemy. Did I not fight enough? I knew coping should be wonderful. I had no strength for that. If I learn to live, when treatment comes to an end…will I get a diploma for being able to cope with life – with all its power? Its strength?

It is so difficult…it hurts…I think I…do I want to live? Maybe I do…please do not leav me, I will try…I want to learn more.

At that hospital as well, I felt different from all the other patients. Most of the adolescents there were of a lower socioeconomic status. Most of them were younger than I was. They were still attending high school, while I had already graduated. I had the feeling that I needed to step down lower in order to communicate with them. It sounds very arrogant, but no one could speak my language. I had to learn street language, slang, and a different style of life and thinking. Now I think that learning about other people, another way of life, and another class, expanded my experience and enriched me. Without that hospitalization, I don't think I would ever have been able to learn to interact with so many people. We learned from each other, imitating each other's behavior. The way I exhibited my illness was certainly something I learned from them.

So, all along, my closest friend continued to be paper. My writings and drawings were the only outlet for me to actually reveal my real language and style, without criticism. So, I wrote and wrote, and by covering hundreds of pages I gained some sense of relief. In the following, I wrote about my hatred for that place, its white walls, its smell of medications:

> *And he lies there, between white walls*
> *It is so quiet that it shouts, it is burning*
> *He looks aside, he looks back, but never finds anything, not even a*
> *   slight clue*
> *Looking at the corners, maybe there — some hopes — but no*
> *He sees a little hole in the wall, connecting with that in*
> *The heart, burning, not pleasant, threatening to disconnect, to tear, to*
> *   cut,*
> *He lies there, expecting*
> *Who, or what?*
> *Expecting for it to come, for it to arrive, for it to appear*
> *He hears the noise of a window which opens, an old door*
> *So monotonous, no beginning, no middle, no end*
> *No reason, no feelings, just*
> *From time to time hears the sounds of a step, one forward, two back*
> *Unidentified step,*
> *It is their step, theirs, not yours*
> *He lies there, waiting, when it arrives*
> *For whom, or for what*
> *He then decides to get up*
> *Oh, Oh*
> *Things look different*
> *The view is different*
> *He sits, and gets up, tries to understand, wishes to change*

And runs away and you, you there, up there
Answer him, give him an explanation or an answer
Let him be, at last, relaxed
Whether he lies down, sits or stands
Give him the right to live, forever and ever
Forever and never and ever

During the first months in this long hospitalization, when I refused food, the staff would connect me to a nasal tube and/or to intravenous liquids, so I would receive nourishment without eating. Thus, with the eating arena eliminated, other behaviors took on more significance to replace food. I began harming myself and received the diagnosis of a self-destructive person. I could not fight it. In Rome, one needs to act as the Romans do. In psychiatric hospitals, people are crazy and try to kill themselves. So, I joined the club and constantly tried to kill myself. From time to time, I was allowed to visit home for the weekends. When visiting home one time, I collected all kinds of pills and swallowed them. My parents noticed that I became lethargic and realized I was trying to commit suicide. They took me to a regular hospital to pump my stomach, and I slept for three days and nights. Other times, when I was stressed out or depressed, I used to cut myself using a knife, a piece of glass, or other sharp things I'd found and secretly hidden away. Usually I was caught afterwards, and the things were taken from me, so I immediately began collecting new ones. It seems as if, throughout this entire period of time, I was focused on trying to discover chance after chance to harm myself, to lose weight, and die. That kept me busy all day long.

Each day at that hospital looked like the one before, and I fell into the routine. After a while, when I could not stand the intravenous liquids anymore, I agreed to eat. At mealtime, I had to eat because we were under close supervision, and there was no way of getting rid of the food. After breakfast, we were required to participate in a recreational activity. For months, I refused to participate and would not go until I was physically forced. This may seem ironic, because I was a very creative person who loved painting, sculpture, and writing. But they expected me to weave rugs and do all kinds of senseless, stupid, dull crafts. Sometimes I was taken to the hospital school, just because they did not want me to sit around doing nothing all day long. However, the level of material taught was very low, and I found no challenge there either. After lunch, there were treatments, mainly individual psychological treatment or group therapy, and then we had free time until dinner.

I lost track of time. When you live in a closed world with no challenges, no changes, and no demands, you soon get used to it. You start being instead of living, existing instead of fighting. I felt I was riding a train that was racing downhill. My condition, at least my emotional condition, constantly deteriorated. When I think about it now, I can't understand how I did nothing during every day, day after day.

During all that time, I had no connections with friends outside of the hospital. Most of my age group was in the army, and I had never been a very social type outside. I had only one friend from my high school with whom I maintained close contact (and we are still friends today). Hence, my social interactions revolved around the other patients.

Some of the other youngsters' problems really touched me and, like always, I tried to help them. I always could help others more than I could help myself. I used to listen and give them support. The ones I could relate to were youngsters who didn't have a chronic condition but who'd been put there temporarily, like me. As with me, if you saw them on the outside, you'd think they were normal (if there is such a thing). One boy was hospitalized because of post-traumatic stress disorder, which he'd developed while in the army. He was a very nice-looking person, but was always quiet and never spoke with the others. He was miserable, and I had the feeling that he didn't deserve the suffering he was experiencing. He looked like a regular guy on the street who'd been put there by a streak of bad luck. One girl had an obsessive-compulsive disorder and was particularly anxious. Another girl who had a reactive depression after her mother's death was like a catatonic person when hospitalized, but she soon recovered and left.

The worst experience of all, back then, was being isolated. I suffered this degradation twice. Once, when I refused to eat and tried to harm myself, I was constrained to a bed in an isolated room, and they gave me a nasal tube to get some nourishment into me. For two days, I was unable to move – my hands, legs, and head were tied down. The only way the staff could hear me was if I yelled, but I'm not the type of person who shouts. I wasn't allowed to get down to go the bathroom, but I couldn't stand the idea of emptying myself in bed. I couldn't relax and was under so much stress that they gave me an injection to calm me down. It mostly made me sleep. Time halted. When I was more alert, I counted the minutes until I'd be free.

I remember when they let my parents come and visit me in isolation. My mother came in and was shocked and angry. She cried, but she never talked to me – she couldn't share her feelings or support me. I couldn't stand her being there. Immediately after they released the constraints, I wrote:

> *The flowers in my room died*
> *Sad, and lonely*
> *No light reaches them*
> *Not even a ray of sun*
> *They are lonely*
> *Entirely alone*
> *They are just like me*
> *Almost the same –*
> *Almost dead*
> *And by the end – me too*
> *There is no why, there is just because*
> *It happens*
> *Never say anything*
> *All in their heart*
> *Then it will blow over*
> *And so will I*

The second time I spent in isolation did not involve physical constraints. I was not behaving as I should. I wouldn't participate in all
those wearisome, stupid activities. I continued reporting hearing
voices and a wish to harm myself. Therefore, out of concern for me,
they placed me in an isolated room. There was only a bed and a small
window in that empty room. I had nothing with me – they'd taken
my watch. I learned to identify the time of day according to the light
entering through the window. I became sicker and sicker during
those ten days.

It came to a point where I felt that I could no longer live in
hospitals. It seemed to me that I was never really living. I was being
treated, I was on medication, I used to fight with those who wanted to
save me – but I had no time to live. I used to think it was not up to me

Illustration 17 The Destiny of Life

to make decisions. I believed in destiny. I felt it was my destiny to suffer. Someone bigger and stronger than me had decided that this was the kind of life that I must live. How could I fight such a power? My drawings during those long, unending days in the youth psychiatric department illustrate my belief in an external force that made decisions for me. In *The Destiny of Life* (illustration 17), I drew a prone dead female figure. Life went on for the sun (albeit a black one, as usual) and for the tree; yet it was my destiny to die. I was not destined to have a normal life. Whether it was me who cried or others who cried for me, I am not sure, but there are drops of tears in the air above the tree.

Illustration 18 Farewell

Yet it was hard for me to leave life, and I drew this dramatically in *Farewell* (illustration 18) from the same time. This drawing depicted a second female figure, waving and saying goodbye to the dead figure lying there. I am unsure if I was portraying the two different parts within me (one who still wanted to live and the other who wished for death), or if the parting figure was someone else. This time, the figures have faces.

Friday nights were the worst. I knew, that outside, somewhere in the world, people were having their Friday night, Sabbath eve meal together. Youngsters my age were getting ready to go out, to have fun. Whereas, for me, it was just like any other endless, monotonous day:

Friday evening
It is twilight
Another week has passed and gone
Many views, signs, and expectations have passed between the two eyes
And he never stops seeing, anxious, doubly fearing
Everything has gone, passed, gone away
As if suddenly over
Sitting there alone, so pure, so innocent
Only a kid, God, only a kid!
No, he is not winning. He keeps losing. Losing life, losing the world
You let him stay alive – but inside he is dead
You gave him the opportunity to laugh, but he is so sad
You never hit him, but he is in such pain
Maybe for others it is easy, but for him – it is so heavy
And sad, sorry God, for only He cries
A rain of tears, a storm of emotions, a lightning of hopes,
Thunderstorm of facts
They all come together in that darkness
Inside storm, very personal. Against all realities. Refusing to explode.
It is not time yet.
One movement joins the music that is finished for others and
Remains his for eternity, only his
The kid wants, tries, is punished, and tries again, fights, but fails
Keeps trying, keeps walking

The kid loves, but doesn't touch life
Disappointed by reality, he doesn't know
He is crying again
God, do You hear?
God, do You see?
God, do You feel?
Why don't You answer?
Why do You leave him there alone with all those questions?
Why he is so lonely, with no answers?
Why is he so frightened by emotions?
Why he is overwhelmed with facts?
Why did You pick a flower that is already dead?
Why, God? Why?
Friday evening
It is late
The feeling starts and never ends
This is how it is for him – the kid
Only a kid.

Part of my treatment was under the responsibility of a nurse therapist who was assigned to me. She invited me to have personal talks, and she was in charge of my behavioral schedule – assignments, challenges, token economy. Then there were the psychologist and the psychiatrist with whom I had individual sessions. More digging into my head, into my past and my illness. I think they all had the wrong view of what a good client is; they wanted someone ready to share, talk, and discuss all the bullshit. But when a person is under such stress, I really believe that delving into their sorrow isn't the best route. Also, they assumed that recovering would emerge after comprehensively examining each piece of my existing shit. I believed that shit was something dirty that should be thrown away, so why dig into it and peck away at it? Every time I talked about some shit, they were so pleased with me. They celebrated every bad thing I found to say about memories or my parents. It seems as if they were happy when I was behaving sick and stupid. No one treated me as a person, that is to say, as a normal person. Nobody tried to enlist my positive strengths.

Any signs of normalcy were viewed as rejection or objection on my part. Treatment thus strengthened the illness. I was obsessed – well, they were obsessed – with searching my early years for problems at the root of my sickness and with fine tuning my diagnosis. Together, we tried to create a creature who was supposed to be me, who could fit all the diagnoses. But was I only sick? Was there no healthy part within me? No future for me? No outside world, with new opportunities? I was bored with delving inside my shitty self, a process I saw as never-ending. I was sick and tired of all that ill language – the kinds of words and colors in our conversations that were all symbols of illness. And when all you can see is sickness, all you can do is talk about sickness, and all day every day you are only surrounded by sick people – how can you possibly be normal? How can you possibly recover?

I did not see any use for those treatments or for the unit activities. I had to participate in drama therapy and music therapy, but I felt so distant from them. These media didn't speak to me. I couldn't relate. Most of those hours passed with me resistant and quiet. When I did not act in drama because I hated it (but maybe the truth is that, actually, I was afraid of letting others learn about my emotions), it was translated as resistance because of my difficult situation, my suicidal or borderline personality. When I refused to sing because I hated my voice, it was interpreted as another sign of my poor condition.

Except for my assigned nurse therapist, not one member of the staff ever tried to get involved with the things that I liked: writing, reading, and drawing. None of them tried to get inside my world, my preferences. I had to conform to theirs. So, I was my own therapist. I wrote and wrote like someone possessed. They knew I was writing and drawing, but no one wanted to see all my work, and they even asked me to take my drawings away. My writing was considered to be another sign of my inability to interact with others, so eventually they took my pen and papers. But I hid little pieces of crayon and small bits of paper, and I continued writing. If only someone had read what I wrote, they would have discovered that everything was there laid out before them: not only all the problems and the sickness, but also the solutions. But I guess this was not in their textbooks.

You are trying to punish him with what you are doing
But nothing happens to him. Only to you
Look, he will not die, just you
You are angry at him, but he is yours, with you, part of you
He lives, he sleeps, he is healthy, he exists
And you are disappearing, going, and vanishing
You, and just you
Don't do it for yourself if you do not believe enough
Just do it for those you care for
And even if you say you don't know that, inside you,
In your soul, there is some creature. Yes, for him
Now, it will be for him, and later on, for you
All this way isn't worth it
With all the ladders to climb, there are so many to take you down
You go up, but actually go down. Facing the wrong direction
You still have life to live. It's only the beginning
Even though you see the end — you still have life
Give your life the same chance you have been asking from them
Maybe, it will be good again
On that path you take, there will be no one to experience the good
Since you will not be any longer
You deserve happiness. You deserve satisfaction. You deserve a friend
Yes, you deserve, you deserve
If you give it a chance, it might come one of these days
Do not prevent yourself from living. Do not take life away from
    yourself
They want you, although you hate them. You are angry at the whole
    world
But could it be that the world loves you?...
To fight means to win, to compete is to lose
You need the power, the strength, the ability, but most of all the
    decision
To start here and now, together or alone,
To take the rest of you, the rest of me forever

My assigned nurse sometimes read my writings, and she was more optimistic than the others about my future. She was the only one who actually discussed the future with me. She told me of someone who had been in my situation and had come out of it. This nurse was the only one I went to see after I got married, and I brought her a photograph from my wedding.

During this period of my hospitalization, I wrote and wrote as if I was obsessed and afraid of not having enough time to tell all the things I had to. Later on, when therapy with Tammie came to a point where I felt normal and happy, I gave her two presents: a 500-page book, which was the collection of all my writings, and a big collage of the little note-sized drawings I had made during that lengthy hospitalization. But at that time in the hospital, I still felt miserable, and I wrote:

> *The pain is hers — deep deep inside*
> *It is with her, with all of her — the sorrow*
> *It is in her, inside of her — logic*
> *It is with her — along the way — memory*
> *The shining white, the tearing black,*
> *The intimidating red*
> *A spot, a spot, a spot for life*
> *He failed and never got up. Before his day came*
> *He is so young, so young, a cloud*
> *She turns — around and around — the thought*
> *She is there, not here — the tear*
> *She is burning, never stops — the soul*
> *Our part is so small, nothing, but exists*
> *The wish to stand behind, to support, to hear*
> *To give a hand, to give a shoulder, to listen*
> *To take her far away, to give her a smile*
> *In the taste, in the taste of life.*

In those days, writing was the main aim of my life. Everything I did was in order to return to my room, take my papers and pen from their hiding place, and write what I felt during that day. Everything else was vague. Writing was all that mattered. In reading these writings today, it seems that each day, then, I grappled with the same issues. The same conflicts between the life and death wishes. But, I can see that I did have the strength to invest an inordinate amount of creativity into finding new and different ways to express those same ideas:

> *You gave me a hand but I never took it*
> *You try to give me, but I could not believe*
> *You opened a little window which I closed*
> *You took me closer to you, but I went away, to the corner*
> *You took me, you sent me forward*
> *But I kept walking in the same place, not moving*
> *I stepped over the problem*
> *You tried to teach me about existence*
> *And I pulled toward death*
> *You smiled even while being sad*
> *It is not because I don't want to*
> *It doesn't mean this is the end*
> *I took you with me, to cherish, to remember*

I was also drawing profusely. In my drawing *The Prayer* (illustration 19), using the same black and white colors and the same kind of old paper, my depression is obvious. Black clouds permeating all around, and I stood on a bridge, perhaps most symbolic of suicidal thoughts. But, remarkably, I also had hope. I hoped things could improve and be better. With outstretched arms, in a strange twist, I turned to God, to some external source of help, to appeal for change in my life. It is amazing that, as difficult as my condition was, I never completely gave up. I cannot explain how this happened, but as I went plummeting down and down and down with my depression, the hope and prayer started. Maybe this occurred because, when nothing could get worse, there was no alternative; either things had to start improving, or else I had to stop being. I guess I felt this was no longer a game. I had to choose between life and death – and I chose life. I started developing hopes, desires, and wishes.

Illustration 19 The Prayer

It was more than seven months after my arrival at this hospital that I began to spend most of my time trying to persuade my parents to get me discharged. My parents were convinced that I was dangerous to myself and others, so they refused. Only after I warned them that I would die if I stayed there – that I would kill myself – did they agree to let me come home. The psychiatrist did not want to discharge me, but I left, eight months after I had arrived. I left the hospital in January of 1994. I was almost 20 years old.

At home, my mother was very anxious, not letting me out of her sight. I had to go with her everywhere – even to the bathroom. After two weeks, I couldn't stand being outside the hospital any longer, and I wanted to go back. Life, and especially life so close to my mother, seemed to be frightening, and my mother's protection was too much for me. Like always, when I was in I wanted out. When I was out I got frightened and wanted back in. I did not know what to do with myself.

Then, one day, I decided that enough was enough. I threw away all my medications. I stopped taking them, and I decided to try and live again. And I started to live. I don't know what helped me. Under medication, I felt big, heavy, and low. Without the drugs, I felt like a new person. I could see the world around me. Being in the real world, I was full of fears, but I could also see some challenges:

I see a little girl crying
And an angel who is sent away from paradise
And an angel being sent away
I am afraid of those who look above and behind
God is there, looking at all He has created
Hey, Mom, look
Give me some strength, power,
Because soon everything is coming to an end
And you should not pick the flowers
I see a little girl crying
Fearing her own shadows
Don't know about eternity
Don't know where the border is
Don't know who and what am I
What do I know, anyhow
See you disappearing
See myself alone
We will be born and go wherever we are led
We will be told why and where
There is some weakness in me and I fall down
I always keep falling
There is a little girl sitting and crying
A neurotic figure
Fearing her own shadows
And I sit and write

Don't know to whom, or why
In half shadow, a quick look
Rain of tears, thunderstorm of disappointment
Extinguishing of emotions. Lightning of hopes
Go away. Give her some answers
A little girl's cry

If my writings were one positive force that helped me recover, the other major one was my dog. When I left the hospital, I felt I needed the companionship of a dog, and my parents obliged me. I think she (I know I'm supposed to call her 'it', but my dog isn't an 'it'; she's an important, loving creature with a soul) helped me recover. Bamby, my dog, gave me a reason to stay at home after I'd left the hospital, and, later on, to leave home and take her for a walk. A great deal of the exposure assignments Tammie gave me were related to my ability to go out of the house and take my dog for a walk, each time for a longer distance, to a more central place, without running away from people. My dog was the first being that I had to take care of; she was someone for whom I was solely responsible. She gave my life significance. In trying to truly take care of someone else, I learned to take care of myself. I got some goldfish as well. I needed to be surrounded by friendly creatures, and the animals were friendly to me. I had a rabbit that delivered bunnies, and I think they helped me a lot.

I still have my dog and find a lot in animals that people lack. Honesty, trustworthiness, friendliness. I do not always find all that in people. My dog is so helpful, so attuned to me. When I used to argue with my husband, she would have diarrhea and vomit. She couldn't stand it. She was also the one to tell me when the time came for me to go to the hospital to give birth to Or. She paced back and forth all that night. She keeps a nightly vigil under Or's bed, and only awakens if I feel bad, and then she wakes up my husband. Only when I am okay does she return to sleep.

Now that I teach a special education class, I hope to bring animals into the class as a mode of helping problematic children express

Illustration 20 Me and You

emotions, accept responsibility, express love and affection, and feel the experience of being loved.

I completed my last drawing, *Me and You* (illustration 20), after I returned home from the hospital and decided that I could actually stay at home. I had decided never again to return to a hospital. In this drawing, it was the first time I could think of myself as with someone. And this someone was a male figure. Not only wasn't this drawing depressive anymore, but, also, one can see for the first time the sex of the figures. A man and a woman. They were not too thin, and they were together. I had begun to wish that maybe, one time, sometime, I would be able to find someone to share my life with.

And now I'll stop relating my own narrative, and let Tammie present things from her viewpoint, in the next part of this book. Later, in Part III, I'll add my comments and thoughts related specifically to what she'll describe.

PART II

The Therapist's Story

The Challenge of Treating Ayelet

I

Getting Acquainted

I first learned about Ayelet when she was 15 years old. Her parents came to my private clinic to consult with me, telling me that they had a daughter with 'some not-too-serious problems, a kind of eating disorder', who was an out-patient in a nearby hospital (her first). At that hospital, she was being treated with medications and group therapy. They wanted me to accept their daughter for treatment, in order to expedite her discharge, but I refused. My refusal was based first on the fact that I was under the strong influence of the need to hospitalize another anorexic girl I was treating. It was a very traumatic experience for me. I had lost many nights' sleep recently, worrying about her, doubting whether there was anything I could do to avoid hospitalization, fearing how she would make it. Second, I thought it was inappropriate to interfere with the staff working at that hospital. Third, I was not really sure that I was being told the whole truth about Ayelet's condition, so I did not want to get involved.

Ayelet and her parents came to me again four years later. They reported that Ayelet had been hospitalized for most of the intervening time in four different hospitals, one of which had been a placement by court order from the district psychiatric court of law. At the time of this meeting with me, Ayelet had been out of the hospital for three months and claimed to be fine. However, she had many problems and urgently needed therapy. The psychiatrist who was treating her at that time was dying, and Ayelet was in a state of crisis from the fear of his impending death. Together, we counted twenty-four different medications she had received over the last six years (three years at home and three hospitalized) and ten different therapists who had treated her. Only a month later, I was able to receive her written diagnostic evaluations and summaries of her hospitalization. Only then did I realize that she had received different, very severe, and varying diagnoses: borderline personality; suicidal personality; anorexia disorder; and a comorbidity of depression and anxiety (American Psychiatric Association 1994).

Yet, even before receiving the medical and psychiatric evaluations about her condition, my inclination was to refuse accepting her for treatment. I felt uncertain as to whether I could help where so many good therapists before me could not. However, I saw Ayelet in my clinic that day in 1994, sitting in the corner as if she were trying to make herself invisible. She was a beautiful, fragile, almost 20-year-old girl, who was nearly smiling and looked almost unreal. The only thing about her that showed vitality and life were her eyes. Big, shining eyes looking at me miserably. On the spot, I felt myself fall in love with this girl. She seemed to me to be brimming with a special inner and outer beauty and grace, despite her afflictions. Now, almost seven years later, she has become much more than a client to me. I care for her dearly. I think I have learned more from her than she has learned from me. We have traveled down a long path together and even now, when she is married, we have finished writing this book, and she is the mother of two beautiful children (a son aged two and a six-month-old daughter), we keep meeting once every two or three months, just to maintain contact.

I treated Ayelet for about four years. I started with joint sessions for her and her parents together in the period after her discharge from the hospital; I counseled her parents; we continued with family therapy; I turned to individual therapy with her; and then I held counseling sessions with Ayelet and her young husband. I think it is worth telling Ayelet's story because it incorporates all kinds of intervention settings (parent supervision, family therapy, individual therapy, and couple counseling) and a wide variety of techniques (verbal therapy, storytelling, imagery, metaphors, exposure, and more). Her story is one of my hesitation and confusion as a therapist, as well as my optimism, faith, persistence, and humanness. It is the story of her coping, fighting, and overcoming as a client. Most of all, I believe her success is the result of our close relationship; our ability to develop collaboration, trust, hope, and belief in each other.

2

Family History

From my earliest encounter with this family, I estimated that an intake interview on their complex family history would necessitate at least several hours. Due to the urgent need to treat Ayelet, I started by collecting only the basic information and then, throughout our work together, I continued gathering details. Even now, during the process of writing this book, after treating Ayelet for several years, I learned some new particulars about her past. For the sake of clarity here, I will present the family history and Ayelet's background as one concise story.

Ayelet is the middle child in a family of three daughters. Her older sister is two and a half years older than Ayelet. This sister was always described by Ayelet as the ideal of success and strength, as someone who knew what she wanted and how to achieve it. This sister played a major role in Ayelet's feelings of competitiveness and worthlessness as a child. At the onset of therapy, this sister was living with a boyfriend and studying at the university, and Ayelet was not on speaking terms with her. Later on during therapy, that sister returned home and, sometime afterwards, got married. Ayelet and her older sister gave birth to children at the same time, and, as we terminated treatment, Ayelet had started developing a nice relationship with her.

The other sister, 11 years younger than Ayelet, was born after the mother had many miscarriages, and this daughter was very pampered. During the years when Ayelet was in and out of hospitals, her young sister did not figure prominently in her life, although the parents reported that Ayelet talked often at the time of her love and concern for her younger sister. As we started therapy, Ayelet frequently felt disturbed about her then eight-year-old sister, worrying that she might be exposed to similar difficulties that Ayelet had been exposed to and would develop a similar illness. Today, as adult and adolescent, they are very good friends.

The mother, 50 years old at the time of their referral, was born in Israel. Her parents are Holocaust survivors from Hungary. Her father (Ayelet's grandfather) spent the war at a work camp near Budapest, gathering the dead people. He met Ayelet's grandmother in Hungary after the war, before immigrating to Israel. The couple spent some time together in Cyprus after their boat was denied entry to Israel, and eventually they managed to immigrate to Israel where they and their children and grandchildren (including Ayelet and her family) live until this day. The family history is still not clear, since it is something they do not wish to talk about, and do not voluntarily share with their children and grandchildren. Ayelet is very close to her grandparents. She respects them greatly and often shares with them things she wouldn't share with her own parents.

I still have very limited information even about the parents themselves. Although they are very nice, cooperative people, they do not talk about themselves. They were each raised in an atmosphere of not sharing emotions or problems with other people, and, even with me, they would not share information unless I asked or even demanded to know details.

Ayelet's mother was a preschool/kindergarten teacher for many years, until around the time we started therapy, when she decided to continue her studies toward a bachelor's degree. She began working in an elementary school, and now serves as the school principal, where she is very successful. She is a good-looking woman who is highly intelligent and very easy to relate to. She is also a very dominant figure in the family. In her relationship with Ayelet, she is very sensitive but at the same time very ambivalent, and often sends double messages. She suffers from many anxieties; however, they do not appear pathological but rather as over-anxious and over-protective behaviors, worries, and fears, relating to the things and people she cares about. She is a perfectionist and obsessed about cleaning and about doing her job the best way possible.

Ayelet's father is a very gentle, quiet man who listens carefully but almost never expresses his opinions. He was a good-looking man at 53 years of age at the time of their referral. He was born in Romania. During Nazi rule, his father was imprisoned, and he was raised by his mother and her sister. He came to Israel at the age of 15 with a group of teenage immigrants. He served in the military for many years and then continued his higher education. He works as an engineer.

Ayelet's History

Ayelet was born prematurely in the seventh month of pregnancy, during the Yom Kippur War. After a difficult breech labor (just as her mother and her son were born), Ayelet had no spontaneous respiration at birth and required resuscitation. She weighed 4 pounds 3 ounces at birth and spent her first month of life in an incubator. Later, her psychomotoric development was slow. She started walking at one year and seven months old, but started talking on time at around one year old. From birth, she had problems with her digestion. She cried and vomited frequently, and she stopped breathing for short times. The parents reported it was not easy to raise her, and they were very tense about her response to anything new. At the age of three, the vomiting and fainting disappeared. She began to love eating, especially junk food, but she was not overweight.

When Ayelet was less than two years old, she was enrolled in the preschool where her mother taught. The mother reported that, as a child, Ayelet always envied the other children for getting her mother's attention, and she used to ask her mother if she loved her more than she loved the other kids who were there. At that time, Ayelet could not stand to be separated from her mother.

In the other years of preschool, Ayelet became accustomed to being among children, but was always very quiet, had only one or two friends, and was mostly occupied with drawing or playing alone. The parents do not remember any specific problems from those years.

Ayelet started school on time, at the age of six. Throughout elementary school, Ayelet was a very good student. She always completed her homework assignments on time and was very responsible. There was no disobedience problems, and her parents were very pleased by her good grades. Relating to social relationships in those years, Ayelet was liked by her classmates but did not initiate many social connections. Most of her social interactions transpired over the telephone. She used to go to the class parties, but mainly kept to herself.

The parents described her as someone who was always very dependent and constantly in need of physical touch. She wanted her mother to hold her hand or hug her; she always needed proof of being loved.

Development of the Illness

The history of Ayelet's illness began with her dieting at the age of 14, which began from an initial weight of 123 pounds and would drop to a weight of 93 pounds at the worst time. After Ayelet's first 22 pound loss and cessation of menstruation, the school counselor raised her concerns in a talk with Ayelet's parents. I tried to understand how and why Ayelet's parents refused to cooperate with the school counselor and did not agree to take Ayelet to therapy then. When I asked them about this, they answered that Ayelet had always been concerned with her eating, and that they thought the counselor at school was too anxious. They did not believe Ayelet was anorexic, and for a long time Ayelet actually deceived them. Some of their sorrow related to the fact that they were not aware of her serious condition earlier. The couple related how they often argued whether she was really sick or just pretending to be. Only while listening to them could I understand how difficult it was for these parents to accept the fact that their beautiful, smart daughter was ill. In addition, after getting to know Ayelet better later, I learned how manipulative she could be, how convincing she could sound, and how good she could be in deceiving others. Therefore, it took time before the parents realized that she was in a difficult situation and could no longer ignore her anorexic behavior.

The ensuing treatment history included a long list of hospitals and treatments that were ineffective in generating a behavioral stabilization of her weight and testified to a gradual systematic deterioration in her emotional, behavioral, and social functioning. Ayelet started treatment in group therapy and, at the same time, her parents attended a parents group in the psychiatric unit of a general hospital. The parents' talked about how difficult it was for them to be part of this parents' group. They could not identify with the other parents and did not feel it helped them at all. As Ayelet left her group and started individual therapy at the same hospital, the parents described their feelings as moving from anger to empathy, from hope to helplessness. They admitted that, when they understood that Ayelet was not improving, they thought it might be because of the setting. They feared that Ayelet, a sensitive girl, would only learn to imitate other psychiatric patients and become sicker.

Her parents sent her to a third type of therapy, to a private psychologist who applied a very strict eating regimen. They hoped that there, with a more pleasant atmosphere on the one hand, and a very strict eating program on the other hand, she might recover. Indeed, Ayelet gained 18 pounds, and her parents agreed to stop therapy. For a while, they were sure Ayelet had recovered. They were especially fooled by the fact that she continued being a good student. They thought that getting good grades was a sign that she was healthy. When Ayelet started losing weight again, they thought it was because she was studying hard for her matriculation examinations. But then, at the age of 17, Ayelet took an overdose of medications, and they had to hospitalize her. Even then, they could not accept the fact that she had tried to commit suicide and insisted it was an accident; and they insisted on her being hospitalized in a general rather than a psychiatric hospital, where she stayed for two months.

I believe Ayelet's parents denied her illness in part out of shame and fear of stigma, and in part due to their feelings of guilt or self-doubt about their own role in the development of her disorder. At that time, there were many arguments between the parents relating to the question of Ayelet's disorder and whether or not she was really sick. It wasn't until they had again helped release her from the hospital, and were compelled to immediately hospitalize her again in another general hospital, that they began to understand that she was really sick. When they were asked to hospitalize her by legal decree, in a closed unit of a psychiatrist hospital, they were shocked. Ayelet's mother became very frightened, and did not dare disobey the psychiatrist. She insisted on taking Ayelet immediately to the psychiatric hospital. Ayelet's father, on the other hand, was not sure what was best for his daughter, and tried to question this decision. Both were confused and unsure about what to do. Her mother also felt very ashamed and wished to hide these events from everyone she knew. The parents described that month when Ayelet was in the psychiatric hospital as a nightmare, and were happy and relieved when she was released.

Ayelet's parents described the short time that Ayelet stayed at home as a very stressful period. They admitted that they had no idea how to handle her. They argued severely about what would be the right way to go about dealing with her. They also feared that she might influence her younger sister. They shifted between the wish to have her with them and to take care of her, and the wish to have her taken away so that they could try to return to a normal life. They could never rest when she was around, always fearing she would harm herself and never sure how to treat her. Shortly afterwards, Ayelet was hospitalized again in another psychiatric hospital, this time in the adolescence department, where she spent eight months and was in isolation twice.

Ayelet began therapy with me after leaving the last hospital. Since that time, she had no further hospitalizations, nor did she use psychiatric medications of any kind. At first, she still used laxatives and medications to induce vomiting, but soon she ceased these as well.

3

Collecting an Inventory of Ayelet's Problems and Establishing an Initial Treatment Contract

Ayelet's case seemed so complex that I did not know where and how to begin. The list of well-known therapists who had treated her in the past did not help me feel good about my ability to help her, nor did the long list of hospitalizations and medications. However, from the start, some intuitive feeling led me to sense that although Ayelet was confused and seemed to reject therapy, she was also very naive and was hoping to be helped and be able to trust someone. It was also obvious that she was sick and tired of treatment and therapy. Therefore, I thought I should first mobilize her interest and collaboration. I also understood that she was a seasoned expert in techniques and treatments, and she knew what therapists expected her to say. I did not want to become just another name on that long list from her past.

I knew also about the past attempts to change the way Ayelet thought of herself, to persuade her to gain weight, and to induce her to start believing that she was thin. These were some things I did not want to repeat.

What was clear to me was that, in some way during that first session, she made me believe in her positive resources. Early on, I was impressed by her capacities, her creativity, her somewhat innocent view of the world, her wish to be good, and her desire to change. Although Ayelet seemed to be a difficult, stubborn, and rigid client, who survived ten therapists and hadn't been changed dramatically, I could not ignore her strengths and abilities. I wanted to turn those forces around and mobilize them to facilitate acceptance and change, rather than fighting her, measuring her, or trying, myself, to change her.

In that first session with Ayelet and her parents, I laid out my approach, telling her, 'Listen, I am not going to change you or your problems. I believe you are strong enough to do this by yourself. What I *am* going to do is to propose to you that, together, we will try to find out what you wish, what you need, and how you want it. Then, together, we will try to help you fulfill what you wish for yourself.' Ayelet trapped me immediately, asking, 'And what if you find out that what I really want is to die? Will you help me then?' Her parents started shouting, but I asked them not to interfere, and I replied, 'I don't believe that is what you genuinely want, because you've survived so much agony that if you really wanted to die, you could have done so long ago. Instead, I believe you are strong and fighting to live your life your own way, and that is very understandable.' Ayelet smiled and moved her head. I thought that it was a good starting point and we could progress to make a preliminary contract.

Ayelet's inventory of problematic areas, pain, and suffering was so lengthy that I could not find a way to unravel all of the information in order to decide on a treatment plan. As I had no idea where I wanted to start her therapy, and I knew there were a multitude of problems, I decided I must introduce some order by selecting how to begin and how to end. I view therapy as a planned, designed process, and I believe that due attention should be paid by therapists to the construction of the intervention process (Ronen 1997a).

Using Gambrill's 12 steps of intervention as guidelines (Gambrill, Thomas and Carter 1971; see the detailed description in Part V of this book), I began to design how I would conduct Ayelet's therapeutic process. The first step in that procedure comprises making an inventory of problem areas, based on the rationale that such an inventory will help draw up a profile of the client's difficulties.

I told Ayelet: 'I don't need to tell you that you have enough problems for ten therapists. In order for me to find my way through, I need some help. So let's draw a map of the difficulties you face in all the areas of your life and try to assess what's going on.' It took us the whole session, but together, we compiled the following description:

1. Personal problems

    (a) Eating disorders
    Ayelet is afraid of gaining weight, vomits after she has eaten, uses too many laxative medications, withholds bowel movements, and cannot eat in her family's presence.

    (b) Fears, anxiety, and obsessive-compulsive disorder (OCD)
    Ayelet cannot walk in the street, is afraid to go out alone, and cannot ride a bus. She demonstrates obsessive-compulsive disorder, manifested mainly as a counting compulsion but also as obsessive thoughts, believing that she is harming everyone who is in close contact with her. (As an example, she told me about her grandmother who died, and about the psychiatrist with whom she was very close and who was dying from a brain tumor.)

    (c) Self-acceptance and self-evaluation
    Relating to her emotions, Ayelet feels hopeless and helpless, bored, and lonely. She thinks she is worthless and describes overwhelming feelings of anxiety, fear, depression, and sorrow.

2. Vocational problems

    As Ayelet has not attended school regularly for several years, she has lost confidence in her ability to learn a profession. She wants to study but is afraid of doing so and feels incompetent.

3. Social problems

   Ayelet has been away from home for many years and has not participated in social activities or maintained social contacts throughout most of her adolescence. Most of her friends are girls from the hospital. She is ashamed to try and communicate with her old friends, fearing what they might think of her, and feeling that she does not know how to start connecting with others. Ayelet is afraid of meeting new people, and she avoids social contact.

4. Family problems

   Much blame, suspicion, anger, and guilt feelings of all the family members toward one another are evident. Her parents are not sure how to handle Ayelet, shifting from being afraid to harm her and treating her as if she were made of glass, to blaming her for ruining their lives.

This was only a preliminary list, and we could have added much more, but Ayelet was frightened by its length, so I decided to stop at that time.

A Preliminary Treatment Contract

I next continued with Gambrill *et al.*'s (1971) second step of intervention – problem selection and contract (see the detailed process in Part V of this book). I suggested we start from the 'easiest thing' first: the family relations and roles. My impression was that, although there were many mixed feelings in the family, they really cared for each other and could support each other. Also, I thought Ayelet would need a great deal of help and a reliable support system to contribute to her coping outside the hospital. I also realized that the parents were very confused, felt frustrated, and were not sure how to treat Ayelet. Therefore, I shared my impression with them, proposing that we begin treatment in two settings: parental supervision and family therapy. I recommended incorporating individual therapy with

Ayelet only as we progressed. I believed Ayelet would thus be helped by her parents, facilitating change. I felt she needed to start going out and doing things rather than staying home all day alone, and that by being involved in family intervention she would progress. Ayelet and her parents agreed to this problem selection (comprising the third step in the 12-step procedure).

There were, however, some preliminary guidelines I knew I had to have. I knew that in order to treat Ayelet confidently, I must be convinced that she was not in danger of losing more weight or risking her life. I therefore demanded two conditions for treating her: regular check-ups by a physician and examination by a psychiatrist per need. Ayelet promised in our treatment contract to meet the family physician for monthly check-ups. This would ensure that her weight was appropriate and that she was functioning well physically. I also insisted on her agreeing to undergo examination by a colleague of mine – a child psychiatrist whom I trusted – whenever I felt the need for consultation. During the first six months, I turned to him twice. The first time she was completely confused and seemed to be psychotic, and he thought this was due to changes in electrolyte homeostasis in her brain as a result of her previous starvation. The second time he took her off all medications, thinking she could function well without them. We never consulted him again after that second visit, and as I mentioned above, Ayelet never used medications again.

We decided that we would not talk about her eating habits as a focus of therapy, but that at the end of each session she would briefly report what was happening during the week in that domain and whether there was any change in her eating disorders.

4

Rationale for the Decision to Treat Ayelet Using Multi-Targeted Cognitive-Constructivist Therapy

I decided to design a cognitive-behavioral intervention. The treatment was directed at three main issues:

1. Ayelet's anxiety-related disorders (obsessions, compulsions, anxiety, and fears), which had developed during the hospitalizations.

2. Her skill deficits (lack of a vocation, lack of social relationships, and conflict in family relationships), which had increased in part as a result of her hospitalizations.

3. Her misconceptions relating to herself and the world, which had always been a part of her, and were chiefly responsible for the development of the anorexia.

I thought cognitive-constructivist therapy should be the treatment of choice. I conceived cognitive-constructivist therapy as the umbrella approach that would facilitate the application of different techniques for Ayelet's different problem areas. I planned to incorporate a family intervention to improve her familial relationships and resolve family conflicts (Foster and Robin 1988); exposure techniques to eliminate the obsessive-compulsive disorder (OCD) (Marks 1969, 1978, 1987; Salkovskis 1996); exposure and skill acquisition to reduce fears and anxieties (Rachman 1997; Ronen 1996; Thyer 1991); social skills training to help her in vocational and social situations (Hops and Greenwood 1988; Thyer 1991); self-control intervention

(Ronen 1994, 1995) to promote the acquisition of coping skills; and cognitive-constructivist methods to change her way of thinking, feeling, and behaving, with a special focus on her self-acceptance (Mahoney 1991, 1995; Ronen 1994, 1995, 1997b; Ronen and Rosenbaum 1998; Rosenbaum and Ronen 1998).

This multiple-treatment design that encompassed crucial life skills and targeted the client as well as her environment aimed to empower Ayelet (Mahoney 1991, 1993) by imparting to her the range of skills she needed to help herself (Ronen 1995, 1997b). I expected that cognitive-constructive therapy as the treatment of choice would enable me to help Ayelet help herself, rather than making her feel helpless, weak, and dependent on the therapist. Early on, I identified my major objective in treating her in terms of attempting to try and show Ayelet that she was strong, that she could make decisions about her life, and that it was up to her to make something out of 'all the mess' she had experienced. I believed that by working with her, mobilizing her strengths and resources, and utilizing her creative way of thinking, we could reach the goals of helping her find the 'real Ayelet' – a beautiful, sensitive, intelligent, strong girl.

5
Specifying Target Behaviors and Measuring Baseline Functioning

The fourth step in the intervention process comprises specification of target behaviors related to the specific selected problem areas (Gambrill *et al.* 1971). In this step, details are specified about each selected behavior problem, in order to demonstrate what maintains and reinforces the behavior. The following, fifth step consists of determining the baseline level of the targeted behaviors. Kazdin (1982) emphasized the importance of baseline information for validating the data collection, and for ascertaining in depth all the antecedents, maintenance, and outcomes relating to the behavior. In our intake session, I asked Ayelet to observe herself over the next two weeks with regard to each of the major problems that we had identified and to rate the intensity and frequency of each. I thought these records would provide baseline data and would enable decision making as to where and how to begin therapy. Her parents were also asked to chart Ayelet's different disorders for the same two-week period. They were asked to note whether the problem appeared or not, and to rate its frequency. Ayelet also rated the problems on relevant self-rated comfort scales of 0 to 10.

For the purpose of these baseline records, we divided her problems into several topics: eating disorders; family interactions; OCD; anxiety and fear; vocational study or work; social interaction; and, finally, feeling good about herself.

Eating disorders

The first issue – Ayelet's eating disorders – was viewed similarly by all three respondents (Ayelet and her mother and father). They all reported that during the previous two weeks, Ayelet refused to sit down and eat with the family. Ayelet reported that she still vomited when she ate (at least once a day), used too many laxative medications (daily), and withheld bowel movements. The only time she was willing to join the family for a meal was on Friday nights, when her grandparents came over for dinner.

Family problems

Ayelet was asked to rate the family atmosphere on a self-rating scale ranging from 0 (coldness, indifference, no physical touch) to 10 (happiness, love, affection, physical touch like hugging and kissing). Ayelet reported that between five and six times each week there had been occasions of shouting and snapping at each other, as well as noted feelings of suspiciousness, frustration, helplessness, and distrust. The parents agreed with her report. The father said he had not spoken with Ayelet beyond 'hello' and 'goodbye'. The mother recounted talks related to functional needs. Ayelet reported: 'No honest talk with them.' No one reported any physical touch, and the atmosphere did not surpass a rating of '3'.

OCD, fear, and anxiety

Ayelet's anxiety prevented her from functioning normally. Ayelet reported she was anxious for most of the day, rating her anxiety between 1–3 on a scale of 0 (very anxious) to 10 (very calm). Her obsessions were focused mainly on the fear of a death among her loved ones. Her compulsions revolved around constant counting, especially when she saw by chance something written on death or dying in the newspaper, or when she accidentally thought of something bad that could happen to her relatives.

Ayelet's anxieties and fears severely restricted her behavior. She was afraid to leave home. Her parents reported that she did so only to take her dog out for a walk. Even then, she remained close by the house, and walked only at night when no one could see her. Ayelet added that when she had to leave the house, she would only walk with her dog on the far edge of the sidewalk, mostly in deserted places. She reported crossing the street if people were approaching, to avoid social contact. She was afraid to use public transportation.

Vocational problems

Ayelet wanted to study but was afraid to do so and felt incompetent. For her baseline records, Ayelet was asked to write down whether she did anything relating to a future occupation, such as looking at the classifieds in the newspaper, making telephone calls to inquire into such advertisements, going to her school to ask for her graduation records, taking an examination for acceptance to a course of study, etc. However, during those two weeks she had done nothing but sit at home. She was not even ready to think about studying, and this un-readiness only raised her anxiety.

Social contacts

The only youngsters with whom Ayelet had any relations during the previous four years were friends from the various hospitals. During the baseline period, she had no social contacts. She never called a peer, never received a telephone call, and never left home to go to a party, a movie, or a friend's house.

Self-evaluation and self-acceptance

Ayelet felt hopeless and helpless, bored, and lonely. She thought she was worthless and could not stand herself. These feelings appeared in her charts daily. The most severe emotion charted down was her feeling of emptiness and the thought that there was nothing good waiting for her in the future and, therefore, that there was no hope in life. Still, she did not present any thought of suicide or wish to die.

The analyses of the baseline data enabled our continuation into the sixth step of intervention: the identification of problem-controlling conditions. This step helps identify the conditions preceding and following the problem's occurrence, in order to make decisions about the beginning of treatment (Gambrill *et al.* 1971; Kazdin 1982). At this stage we were ready to begin therapy.

Steps 7, 8, and 9, relating to the beginning of intervention, consisted of: assessment of resources one has in the environment and within oneself; specification of behavioral objectives for intervention; and formulation of the treatment plan (Gambrill *et al.* 1971) (see the detailed description in Part V). Our treatment plan (step 9) included the kind of disorders we would address, the sequence of treatment, the way therapy would be conducted, and its structure in terms of her agreement to meet her family physician for monthly check-ups and to visit a child psychiatrist per need. Throughout the intervention process, we continuously monitored outcomes to furnish feedback on effectiveness and to enhance Ayelet's motivation (step 11) and took steps to maintain the changes achieved (step 12).

As we had decided, we began with family intervention.

6

Family Intervention

The family meetings were conducted in ten family sessions held twice weekly with Ayelet and her parents. Although she had two sisters, Ayelet and her parents did not want them to be involved and rejected my attempt to invite them to join us, emphasizing that 'they are not part of this'.

Foster and Robin's (1988) proposal that negative emotions are both a product and a component of a maladaptive interaction style corresponded aptly to Ayelet's family. The family intervention, therefore, aimed at helping the family members deal with those negative emotions, learn to express their feelings, and change their communication styles.

I used Foster and Robin's (1988) methods of working with families. In one method, the family members were asked to present a problem and then to look for regularly recurring sequences of family interaction that adequately depict the presenting problem within the overall context of the way in which their family operates. These three family members tended to blame each other for their distress and to feel a great deal of fear of and anger toward one another. In these sessions, they learned to express feelings, to practice talking directly to one another, and to look directly into each other's eyes. Later, they were assigned to do things together as a family, such as going to movies and on walks, without mentioning or talking about 'the problem', referring to Ayelet's sickness and hospitalization. They also practiced demonstrating physical affection (touching each other's arms, holding hands, hugging).

A second method consisted of working on a meaningful answer to the question: 'What is each member of the family getting out of the recurring treatments?' At first, they shouted at each other and cried, with Ayelet saying, 'This is hopeless. Nothing will come out of this.' Gradually, they began to talk and to have real, open conversations with each other.

At first, it was difficult for all three family members to talk about their feelings. Ayelet especially blamed her parents for putting her in the hospital. She shared with them the fears she felt then and yelled at them for abandoning her there to be alone and lonely. Her parents wept while talking about how helpless they had felt, how they had been afraid they would lose her, and how they had been ready to do anything in order to keep her alive. They revealed to her and to each other how they blamed themselves for the development of her problem, and they described how they had been constantly oscillating from distress and despair to hope, and back again.

In these sessions, Ayelet would direct herself to me, referring to her parents in the third person (e.g. 'He just left me there...'). She would say to me, 'I'll leave the room, and I want you to ask them what they really feel about me. They won't say if I'm here.' Nevertheless, as I modeled sharing difficult feelings, they began to do so. I asked Ayelet to sit in front of her parents, look directly in their eyes, and tell them directly what she felt. During the first two family sessions, she left the room in the middle, telling her parents she would wait for them outside. In the third session, she said she was ready to talk with her mother but not with her father. I saw Ayelet had an enormous amount of complaints but was afraid to talk about them. She accepted my suggestion that she stand up and say everything she had to say against her parents, all at once, and get it over with.

We had a very difficult fifth session when each of them turned to the other, spurting out what made him or her the most angry. There were tears, anger, and shouting.

In the sixth session, I asked all of them to write letters to each other, telling one another about their wishes and fantasies. At first, Ayelet wrote to her father: 'I wish you yourself would stay in a mental hospital for one month.' But, as we progressed that day she could write: 'I wish you would understand me better' and later on: 'I wish you could teach me how you were able to be so strong and to put up with me all that time.'

It was at that stage of the treatment that I began suggesting that they start doing things together as a family. They were instructed to go to movies and on walks, without mentioning or talking about 'the problem'. Gradually, the family seemed to be beginning to function as a family again. Ayelet never stopped criticizing her parents for their previous behavior, but at the same time she could admit how difficult she was to relate to, and that she would not have known what to do if she had been in their place. She could also say that it was not their fault that she was anorexic, and that she could accept and agree with their need to hospitalize her, although it was a very traumatic experience for her.

As they progressed, they were able to talk about their feelings not only in my presence but also at home. After the first ten meetings, Ayelet began individual therapy, and we continued meeting as a family once every six to eight weeks to deal with issues that arose.

7

Parent Counseling

Throughout the first year of treating Ayelet, I met with her parents once every three to four weeks for a consultation and supervision session. I started counseling them as we finished the family therapy and I started seeing Ayelet individually. We discussed how to deal with her various behaviors, how to respond to her eating habits, to what extent she could be asked by them to take on responsibilities in the house, and how to increase her independence. The parents were very confused, wanted help, and did their best to follow my suggestions. They tried to help her feel welcome at home and return to 'normal family life'. Often, they would call me to consult on how to deal with specific incidents, especially when something in her behavior frightened them. However, though Ayelet did not eat normally yet, she did not wish to die. Gradually, they realized her life was no longer in jeopardy, and they started trusting her, interfering less in her life, and allowing her more independence.

During the parents' sessions, we looked at the family relations. According to her parents, Ayelet was angry with them both, but she felt it much easier to accept her father's way of behaving than her mother's. She was very close to her mother, and she viewed her mother's 'abandoning her at the hospital' as a betrayal. Ayelet could not talk with her mother about this, but the mother sensed it, and found it difficult to talk in the sessions about what it had been like for her to hospitalize her daughter. The parents reported that Ayelet was also angry because her 'sickness' was a secret kept from people, and she felt her parents were ashamed of her.

The mother's intellectualization and emphasis on a cognitive pattern of thinking and behaving were striking to me, and were completely different from Ayelet's emotional patterns. I utilized a situation which could enable a good starting point to bridge the mother–daughter gap by dealing with the anorexia from an intellectual distance. The mother was in college and consulted me about her wish to write her final assignment on anorexia. I thought it was a good opportunity to collaborate with Ayelet.

The assignment included interviewing her daughter, reading about the disorder, and sharing her own feelings. These helped her accept the problem of anorexia as one which was shared by other people. Instead of blaming herself, the mother found a sense of achievement and joy in the fact that they had overcome the disorder and made it out of the hospital with a healthy, living daughter. The mother was required to interview Ayelet for many hours, in an attempt to learn from Ayelet's point of view what her experiences and feelings had been. Both of them cried and opened up, enabling a shift from communicating on an intellectual level to an emotional one. Trying to understand themselves and the problem better, they became ready to accept and forgive one another, in a wish to develop a new relationship. When they finished, they gave me a copy of the assignment.

The father, also, learned to express his love for Ayelet (by holding her hand, smiling at her, not criticizing her). As he followed my instructions not to talk about her problems but rather to find other common areas to talk and share feelings about, their relationship improved remarkably.

8

Beginning Individual Therapy with Ayelet

About nine weeks after the family came to me, following the initial family treatment and separate parent counseling, I started treating Ayelet individually. I obtained Ayelet's agreement to meet with me for weekly individual sessions. I also made myself available to her by telephone between sessions. As we initiated this stage of therapy, Ayelet was very suspicious and cynical, did not trust me, and often gave me the feeling she was not there at all. She was talking, and on the surface everything sounded fine, but I did not feel any emotion, as if her mouth and head were detached from her pain and her feelings.

As our relationship developed after about six more weeks, I felt we were becoming closer. Then, Ayelet stopped coming to sessions. After three weeks, I contacted her and she came into the clinic. It emerged that Ayelet had disappeared because of her obsessive thoughts. She was living under the impression that she had the magic power of harming and hurting people she cared about. She gave me as proof what she had done to her own family, her grandmother, and her previous therapist who had recently died. I realized that she was terrified of harming me too, because I had now become someone important to her.

With this understanding, I tried to persuade Ayelet that my magic powers were stronger than hers. I explained that while she was helpless and surrendered to her thoughts and could not control them, I, on the other hand, had the power of controlling my thoughts and having them obey me. She replied that she was crazy, and that she had been told this in the hospital. She cited as evidence her tendency to hear voices as only crazy people do. I redefined her 'craziness' as an inside voice, the voice of her thoughts that she would hear. I described how each of us hears our own internal voices, which are our wishes, fears, and confusion, and how we can learn to change those thoughts. She was doubtful, but the fact that I did not send her to a psychiatrist and that I remained calm made her think she might be ready to try to change her thoughts. She agreed to return to therapy.

I taught her about the way all of us talk to ourselves all the time. This self-talk directly arouses emotions and behaviors. When someone says 'I can't help it, I'm afraid. This will never work', then stress and anxious feelings will arise. However, we can learn to use self-talk in a positive way, to improve our coping, and to change our automatic negative self-talk. For example, one can tell oneself instead: 'I know this is difficult, but I hope that if I try I might be able to do it. Maybe I'll be a little afraid, but, if I don't run away, the fear will lessen.' Such self-talk might help stop unwanted thoughts and start a better, more helpful way of thinking. We practiced the method of changing automatic thoughts to mediated ones, and Ayelet had to practice at home as well, looking for at least one example of a thought she could try to change each day. She thought it was artificial. Still, I asked her to try do so, and gradually it became more natural for her.

I believe that one of the most important steps toward change relates to the therapeutic relationship. As a cognitive-constructivist therapist, I do not consider the therapeutic relationship to be the most important feature in the change process. Nevertheless, I am convinced, as Safran and Segal (1990) stated, that interpersonal relationships formulate the crucial basis upon which we design and conduct the treatment. Trust, empathy, and beliefs constitute the foundation for facilitating motivation, increasing compliance, and enabling a good collaboration between client and therapist (Kanfer and Schefft 1988; Mahoney 1991; Rosenbaum and Ronen 1998). At this stage in Ayelet's treatment, I could assert that we were successfully developing a good therapeutic relationship and were engaging our mutual strengths in the change process.

9

The First Problem Area

Treating Her Obsessive-Compulsive Disorder (OCD)

As mentioned above, we started individual therapy in the ninth week of intervention (after one intake session, two baseline weeks, and five weeks of family therapy). The initial problem selected for treatment was Ayelet's OCD. Until we started treating it, no change had occurred in the pattern of the OCD. Shafran (1998) reported that OCD among children and adolescents relates mainly to the fear of death and danger to the close family. Likewise, Ayelet's anxious thoughts generally involved a fear of her beloved ones' dying. Her compulsions were mainly characterized by counting. Ayelet would count in groups of three, back and forth, in order to change the meaning of her bad or obsessive thoughts. The number of times she had to count depended on how strong the obsession was and to whom it was related. Also, she avoided looking at newspaper obituaries or at the traditional death announcements posted near houses in mourning, because she tended to 'see' the names of the people she loved inside the black frames.

As suggested by Salkovskis (1996) and Rachman (1997), treatment of OCD is usually based on behavioral components, with no emphasis on cognitive components. I decided to treat her OCD using Marks' (1969, 1978, 1987) method of exposure. The treatment included three stages. The first target was to avoid talking about her obsessive thoughts of harming her family or that they might die. Marks described the process whereby obsessive individuals talk about their distressing thoughts, looking for reassurance, and whereby the environment comforts them, decreasing their anxiety. However, they then become more and more dependent on the environment for future reassurance, which in turn increases the obsession. I explained to Ayelet that talking about her obsessions was like watering a weed. As we water it, it grows, but we want it to die, so we should avoid watering it. I told her that, from now on, I would be the only one with whom she should talk about these things.

The second stage consisted of making an audiotape of Ayelet's thoughts. Marks explained that, while talking to others, an obsessive person believes his or her thoughts seem to be very logical. However, listening to a tape creates the effect of someone else talking, and soon the thoughts become boring and annoying. When the client feels bored and tired of the thoughts, he or she is ready to stop the automatic thinking and begin more palatable mediated thinking. This procedure proved very difficult for Ayelet; she felt stupid both making the cassette and listening to it at home. At first she complained that the recording showed exactly what she felt. These were her true thoughts; therefore, it would not be a helpful method for her. Then, she called me and said she could not stand listening to it any longer, and she hated me for making her do it. I only released her from listening to this first tape after she initiated and recorded a new one: 'I prepared a better cassette – one where I tell nicer things about myself.'

The third stage comprised two components: avoiding the compulsive behaviors while intentionally arousing the obsessive thoughts. As a first step, she was forbidden to count. Cleverly, she initially managed this by simply avoiding meeting people she cared about. She stayed in her room, avoided her parents, wouldn't come to our sessions, etc. When I realized her strategy, I spoke to her by phone and asked her to purposely meet everyone she was afraid of harming as often as she could each day – but to avoid the counting. I brought to our next session as many obituaries as I could find, forcing her to look at them and read them aloud but to avoid counting. Her anxiety increased at first, but shortly it decreased, and after three weeks of practicing, she could meet loved ones and look at death announcements without fear and without counting.

Ayelet used to say she thought she was crazy because she heard voices telling her to count. I reframed this into: 'You're afraid of hurting people, so you think of ways to prevent the possibility of harm.' She liked the reframing of 'hearing strange voices' to her 'internal thoughts that each of us have', and she talked a great deal about how she used to fear being schizophrenic. I asked Ayelet to chart the urge to count daily and to rate how difficult it was for her to avoid it.

As in so many other arenas of her life, when Ayelet decided to overcome her OCD, she always did more than I asked, trying to be perfect. In the past, she had been such a 'perfect' anorexic that no one could treat her or help her change her eating habits. Now, she was taking on more assignments than necessary; for example, when asked as homework to look at mourning announcements three times a day, she would look at them five times.

Ayelet's compulsive counting behavior had disappeared very quickly (within one month), but she was still complaining of obsessive thoughts. She asked for techniques to avoid thinking or else to change her thoughts, but I judged it would be better for her to try to concentrate on those thoughts, to face them until they stopped causing anxiety reactions. I taught her methods to sit down and concentrate on thinking about death and harm. Slowly, gradually, over the next three weeks, these thoughts decreased significantly. About three weeks later, as she practiced ways to overcome her anxiety, she reported that she did not see herself as having OCD any longer.

10

Treating Her Anxieties and Fears

Together with her OCD, Ayelet exhibited a range of anxiety reactions, mainly related to meeting other people. Part of her anxiety could be explained by the long, three-year period of hospitalization and by her withdrawal from social activity for the three years prior to that, at home. She had, in fact, not been involved in normal social activity at all during her adolescent years and exhibited a social skills deficit. Most of the youngsters in the hospital had been younger than Ayelet, came from a different social class, and were not as intelligent. Even at her worst time, when she was on high doses of medication, Ayelet was the best student in the hospital school. The staff complained that she was not friendly and would not take part in social activities; however, I believe that they could not understand how different Ayelet was from the other adolescents there. She did not speak their language, she did not enjoy their jokes and stories, and she was occupied by different kinds of thoughts.

Although the OCD had decreased, no change was apparent in the other anxiety disorders. Ayelet was afraid of walking in the street because she feared people would see she was different. She would not take public transportation or start talking with anyone in the street (even people she knew). She always thought people were looking at her and laughing at her. I personally thought Ayelet looked wonderful – tall, pretty, with long hair, very bright and talented. At first, I used to remark 'How wonderful you look' when she arrived for sessions, but, realizing that this was not a compliment for her, I stopped commenting on her appearance.

At 12 weeks of intervention, we started working on eliminating her fear and anxiety. Although anxieties and fears are commonly found among children (Kendall 1985, 1994; Thyer 1991), disorders in this domain have been shown to be long-lasting and damaging to children's healthy adjustment (Kendall 1994; Thyer and Sowers-Hoag 1988). Anxiety pinpoints distorted rather than deficient cognitive processes (Kendall 1985; Ronan and Deane 1998; Ronan and Kendall 1991). Ayelet possessed the skills necessary for planning and engaging in problem solving. However, when it came to looking at her anxiety, these distorted processes came into play. Her distorted thoughts related to an exaggerated focus on self and an overconcern with the evaluation of herself and others. Treatment of her anxiety, therefore, required not only behavioral exposure techniques (Marks 1987; Ronen 1996; Thyer 1991), but also cognitive skills acquisition for helping her change her distorted thinking (Thyer 1991) as well as self-control training in appropriate self-evaluation and expectations (Ronen 1994).

The behavioral exposure treatment included (Marks 1987):

1. rational explanations concerning the need for her to be exposed to the threatening stimuli and to stop her avoidant behavior (i.e. leaving the house, going out, meeting people, riding public transportation)

2. pinpointing her exposure targets

3. rating her anxiety level before, during, and immediately following exposure

4. remaining in the feared situation until her anxiety decreased. To this end, I asked her to start taking walks outside, and I asked her parents to drop her off several blocks from my clinic and have her walk to me alone.

Ayelet was also given daily exposure tasks such as taking her dog for a walk in ever-increasing distances from her home (first five minutes, then ten, and so on) and in increasingly public, crowded, and noisy directions (from small neighborhood streets to larger roads and then busy thoroughfares). Eventually, she was asked to gradually get used to the bus, until she was able to take it all the way from home to the bus stop near my clinic. Ayelet was instructed to maintain a daily chart of her rate of anxiety before, during, and after each exposure task. She quickly realized that her rate of anxiety decreased when she practiced often, which motivated her to continue working.

The cognitive component included understanding the link between her fearful thoughts and her increase in anxiety, and trying to change the thoughts and to use self-coping methods, cognitive re-structuring, and self-control exercises aims at helping her confront her difficulties and overcoming them (Ronen 1996).

One anxiety-provoking reaction that was difficult to treat was her dreams. Ayelet would sleep fully clothed, fearing that she would be taken to the hospital in the middle of the night. Only after a year in individual therapy, when she was able to follow my recommendation that she return to the hospital and meet with her therapist there, did she overcome her nighttime anxiety. After proving to them that she was alive and healthy, Ayelet no longer had that nightmare, and she started sleeping in pajamas. However, these incidents occurred much later, when she already had a boyfriend who took her to all four hospitals where she had been, in an effort to help her recover from that trauma.

Treatment of anxiety lasted six weeks, in sessions held twice weekly. This stage of treatment was terminated when Ayelet started taking driving lessons (in the 18th week of treatment). After three months of lessons, she received her driver's license.

We were ready to start working on problems relating to vocational and social skills and the environment.

II

Urging Ayelet to Start Studying

It had seemed as if Ayelet needed to overcome her OCD and anxiety reactions as a preliminary step toward starting to learn a profession. When these goals were accomplished, I began to hope she would be able to start planning her life and filling it with contents that would satisfy her.

At the 19th week of therapy, Ayelet no longer suffered from the OCD or her fear of going out, but she still had the hospital-related nightmare. At this time, we started working on her vocational future, which she had not addressed in any way. Ayelet was afraid that people would discover she was 'too stupid' and incapable of learning. She refused to try to do something 'smart'. Also, she feared communicating with people. Vocational problems may be the outcome of skill deficits and of anxiety (Hops and Greenwood 1988). Ayelet's treatment, therefore, focused on both these components. We started looking at newspapers for classified advertisements about work or study. She was instructed to make supported, guided telephone calls to find out details, and to go to her high school to ask for transcripts of her grades. I asked Ayelet to go interview for jobs in which she had no interest – just to practice how to talk and present herself. Then, she agreed to register for a ten-month course as a medical secretary. She was over-qualified for the course, but it provided good practice in riding public transportation, being with people, and taking tests. As I expected, she was the best student in her class and completed the course with honors. However, she still did not believe in herself and found it very difficult when she had to start working as a medical secretary. She feared criticism, failure, and not doing her job perfectly.

Next, Ayelet enrolled in a one-year reflexology course. She would not let anyone else touch her to practice the exercises on her, but always volunteered to practice on others. She enjoyed the course and she finished first in her class.

Following these two courses (two years after starting therapy), Ayelet enrolled in special education studies in college, which was the field she had secretly dreamed of pursuing. The first year of her studies was very difficult; she often threatened to leave and feared failing. Being very honest, frank, and naive, Ayelet, in a dynamic group session for students, talked about her past. The faculty were alarmed, and her adviser recommended that she leave school. Upon Ayelet's request, I contacted the adviser to inquire why, and she tried to persuade me that it would be too dangerous for Ayelet to continue studying: 'She might break down and be hospitalized again.' I felt her instructors were terrified of her. It came to a point where I had to sign a contract where I took all responsibility for her condition and offered to be involved in every aspect of her studies. I urged her instructors to treat her the same way they treated all the other students and not to hesitate in giving her feedback and criticism. During that year, I worked with Ayelet very closely on issues that arose relating to her studies, and I frequently conversed with her academic supervisor. As previously, Ayelet was continually the best student in her special education studies. At the time of this writing, she is working as a teacher, after receiving her bachelor's degree and her teaching permit in special education with high honors. Still, things are not easy for her. She was offered a job, began working as a teacher in a special education school, and received very good feedback from parents and students. However, soon after, the school heard about her past, and they fired her with no justification. Ayelet came to consult with me as to whether or not she should complain and sue them, but together we decided it would not be in her best interests psychologically to become involved then in legal battles in the courts. I was sure she could find another job where she would be much more appreciated. Soon enough, Ayelet did find employment, and now she teaches in a special education class integrated in a regular school, enjoys her work, reveals great sensitivity to her students' needs, and is well liked and respected by teachers, parents, and students alike.

12

Social Skills Training

Social relationships are a very central component in the ability of youngsters to adjust and adapt to a healthy life style. A lack of social skills and social competencies is considered to be a main reason for the development and maintenance of childhood disorders (Hops and Greenwood 1988). During the last decade, there has been an increase of interest in peer relationships among therapists. Also, there is a growing awareness among therapists and researchers of social relationships' influence on healthy adjustment. These recent trends have resulted in concentrated efforts to develop social skills training programs to help children overcome difficulties (Hops and Greenwood 1988).

Ayelet's social competence had improved even prior to direct intervention, during our work toward fear reduction, exposure tasks, and vocational integration. We started working directly on her social skills (Hops and Greenwood 1988; Thyer 1991) in the 24th week of treatment. At that time, Ayelet began studying in the medical secretary course and meeting people through her classes. With my support, Ayelet started improving her social relationships by making phone calls to schoolmates. She continued by going out to the city center and saying hello to old friends she happened to meet on the street. Gradually, she even dared inviting an old friend to come visit her.

In one of her visits to a local shopping center, she met a male friend who lived not far from her, and they started dating. Ayelet was very shy at first, and hesitated whether she should meet him. Several things helped her continue meeting him at that first stage. First, this coincided with the time we worked on social skills, and dating him was a very good opportunity to exercise going out, meeting people, being assertive. Dating thus fit in as part of her training. Second, Ayelet was very lonely and felt she needed close people to be around with. Third, this man, who is now her husband, is a very optimistic, positive-thinking person, with lots of humor. He is also a very persuasive person. As he met Ayelet, he fell in love with her, and didn't let her go out of his sight. Quite soon, they developed a close relationship, very honest and open. So, they started sharing their problems and history. Their relationship became an important part of our sessions. At this time it contributed a lot to Ayelet's social skills training. Later on (as I will describe in the next section), he joined our sessions and it was an important part of working with Ayelet on self-acceptance and ability for sexuality and love. This friend is now her husband. He was, and still is, the principal support system encouraging her to continue her attempts to cope better and to change herself.

13

Starting the Journey Toward Self-Acceptance

Forty-two weeks after the beginning of intervention, we started working toward self-acceptance. Ayelet suffered from insecurity, a lack of self-confidence, and overly critical self-evaluation. However, her tremendous motivation had caused her to begin the process of changing these even before we targeted them directly. As a consequence of her success in overcoming her various anxiety and social disorders, she had slowly been able to feel confident enough to go out and meet friends. She had started showing her grades off with pride. She had even started to put on some make-up for the first time. Still, she found it hard to accept, love, and live with herself. So we started working on her perceptions of the self and the world.

Ayelet's daily language was full of metaphors. She used to say that she was full of garbage and that there was an urgent need to clean this up in order for her to be able to live a normal life. These client-generated metaphors, to use Kopp's (1995) term, introduced by Ayelet routinely as a part of her regular life, served as mirrors reflecting her inner images of self, life, and others. Like Alice in Wonderland, as Kopp proposed, Ayelet could go through the looking glass and journey beyond the mirror's image, entering the domain of creative imagination. Mahoney (1991, 1995) suggested that images could become a key to unlocking new possibilities for self-created change. Slowly, each week, using metaphor sessions, I was able to enter Ayelet's world. I helped her enter the metaphor of cleaning up the garbage, and while imagining herself as a cleaning lady, we looked at all the things we were able to throw away, such as her OCD, fears, and anxieties. Ayelet was happy to notice the expanding garbage can, and said she felt better when she was cleaner.

I felt that the chances of future success would be greater if we took the time to evaluate and assess Ayelet's success over the past year. I felt that helping her to evaluate and appreciate what she had already achieved would increase her motivation and ability to work toward those things she had not yet been able to overcome. In that year, Ayelet's behavior and functioning had changed and improved significantly. She had established friendships and good relationships with her family and had experienced success in school. During that time, she also had ceased vomiting or using laxatives to induce diarrhea. Although she was thin, her weight had remained stable.

After taking time out (several sessions) to review her successes, we started once again to work on those things she was not yet effectively changing. For example, Ayelet continued to find it difficult to eat normally. She would not sit down to the table, and would eat only when no one saw, and only in little bites. She still suffered regularly from stomach aches and used medication to empty herself.

Most of Ayelet's previous therapists had tried to help her change her self-image. Her cognitive therapists had emphasized changing Ayelet's automatic thought of 'How fat I am' into a mediated thought of 'I'm thinner than I need to be'. Her dynamically oriented therapists had translated her eating disorders or body image into symbols of the relationship with her parents. All of these trends had increased her rejection and resistance to change. Ayelet had continued wishing to be thinner than she was, and she still avoided eating unless she felt she was absolutely starving or was being forced to eat by others.

Ayelet's attitude toward herself had not sufficiently changed during the first year of therapy. I felt the need to try something different from what she and her previous therapists had been doing. At first we tried to pinpoint how Ayelet perceived herself by making an 'evaluation circle', an evaluation method used by Wozner (1985). I told her: 'Each of us has many circles of people we know. In each circle, people know us in a different way. The closer they are to us, the more they know about us. So, how about if we learn what people think of you? Let's start with strangers, people on the street – the farthest and most distant circle. If you walk in the street and people you don't know see you, what would they say about you?' Ayelet, after hesitating a bit, replied: 'I think they would say, "Here's a tall, okay-looking girl."' I viewed this as progress because until a few weeks earlier, she could not say anything good about herself. Now she was able to understand that others saw good things in her, but she herself could not yet. The next step would be to help her stop seeing herself so poorly, and the final step would be to assist her in becoming able to accept herself and see herself as a good-looking as well as good-natured person.

We continued with our evaluation circle; I asked her, 'Now, imagine you're being watched by people from your neighborhood. They're not your friends, but they know who you are. What would they say?' Ayelet answered, 'They might add that I'm polite, I greet them nicely. Maybe a bit strange because I always have my head down. But I've changed a lot lately since the time when I lost all that weight and I was hospitalized.'

The next circle consisted of distant or extended family members such as cousins, aunts, and uncles: 'What would they say?' Ayelet smiled and replied, 'Well, they're prejudiced. They think I'm a clever, pretty, wonderful girl who just needs to get rid of some craziness that came over my mind.' I asked her to think what contribution her friends would make to this evaluation, and she answered, 'Too sensitive, very emotional, nice to everyone but herself.'

I then asked Ayelet what she thought of herself, what she would add. She smiled and said very softly, 'I know everyone thinks I am good looking, maybe even beautiful. I already told you that I believe them, maybe they see me correctly and I am beautiful. But I don't feel pretty. I can't help myself from feeling that I'm too fat, and too ugly. I know that's not right, but I still think like that.' Ayelet was also now able to say, 'I know people think I'm smart and pretty, but I feel insecure. I know they're probably right and I'm wrong, but I don't like myself. However…I don't think I'm still thinking of myself as being bad and evil, and I certainly don't want to die anymore. I know I want to live. But I wish I could feel and think about myself those same good things that others do.' We thus discovered the gap between what she knew and what she felt.

We used acceptance methods (Mahoney 1995; Rosenbaum 1999) in order for her to learn to accept and live with herself (Ronen 1997b). As I mentioned before, this tendency of feeling better with herself started even before we treated it. However, in therapy we focused on facilitating a better acceptance of herself, and on changing her passive acceptance into an active ability to love and appreciate herself.

Ayelet repeatedly stated that she had 'some bad things' deep inside her and that she would never recover if we did not deal with them. She often talked about 'the big black hole of nothing', 'falling down into the nothing', and 'a big emptiness inside'. At this stage in the treatment, I asked her to lead me into her big hole. I wanted to learn, together with her, how this 'hole of nothingness and emptiness' looked. I assured her that I could throw her a rope ladder into the hole and help her climb out. This trip was not easy. It involved tears, sobbing, and sorrow. Ayelet thought the 'real issue' to be treated related to her dark hole. I thought that the real issue was the way she did not like herself, and could not accept the way she looked or behaved. I believed that by finding significance to her life, and filling the big hole with self-evaluation and self-love, she would stop feeling empty. I suggested that Ayelet replace the metaphors of emptiness and hole of nothing with the metaphor of gaps. She accepted this idea, demonstrating progress. We defined our next target as helping her accept herself similarly to the way in which others related to her.

In trying to pinpoint what about herself she had difficulty accepting, we realized the issues were related to her appearance, her thoughts, and her emotions. I worked with her toward acceptance of her thoughts and emotions as her one and only irreversible truth, but one with which she had to learn how to live. For example, when she commented on her being too fat, I accepted this belief sadly, 'Well, unfortunately, not all people can be as thin as they want or look as nice as they wish. I am sorry you belong to that group of people, but that's what you are. Now let's see: What does it mean for you to be too fat? How does a fat person feel? How does a fat person walk the street? What kind of thoughts do fat people have? How terrible is it for you to be so fat?'

This response on my part was very unfamiliar to her. However, this approach constitutes what I believe it means to accept the other's person meaning making and to work toward a true understanding of the client's beliefs. Throughout all of her previous treatment experiences, she had been guided toward changing how she viewed herself, and suddenly I did not argue with her, nor did I try to show her the distortions in her thoughts. I accepted what she said, and she did not know how to react. She was silent for a long time, and then she said, 'Well, I always thought that I had to fight in order to be perfect, and that I don't deserve to live if I'm not perfect. I know I'm not perfect, but what you say is that I can still live! I never thought of it like that.' As a next step in enhancing Ayelet's self-acceptance, I introduced my adaptation of the continuum method used by Christine Padesky and Kathleen Mooney, in their Center for Cognitive Therapy in California. The aim of working on such a continuum is twofold. First, it helps clients attain a more realistic perception of their problems. Second, it improves clients' self-evaluation by teaching them how to rate themselves in relation to: others (e.g. peers); a different time in life (e.g. last month); wishes (e.g. the ideal situation or desired behavior); or a different component in functioning (e.g. extent of tics in English versus math class versus recess) (Ronen 1997b). These comparative ratings help the client move from a basic holistic view of 'all or nothing' (which causes one's self-perception as 'a nothing, a failure') to be changed into a view of oneself as lying somewhere in a good position along a continuum of other people or situations.

For Ayelet, I prepared several continua. First, I asked her to rate each of her friends and her family members in relation to 'how good they look' on a scale of 0 to 10. She did not put anyone on 10, but did place one of her cousins at −2. She then regretted doing so, saying, 'No, she also has some good sides. I'll give her a 2.' I asked her to assess what she thought of all these people, and she had mainly good things to say, even about the cousin rated 2. The I asked, 'Could it be that they, too, are not perfect in their appearance, yet they still have reasons to live?'

Next, I asked Ayelet to put herself on the continuum in relation to others, and at first she refused. After a while, she put herself on 7 and laughed. 'Well, maybe I'm even an 8. I don't know.' Ayelet had already stopped looking at herself as an ugly fat girl, but she found it hard to admit that she had better thoughts of herself. I asked her to rate herself on that continuum in relation to her appearance three years ago, in relation to her desired appearance, and in relation to the way she believed she really could look in the future. When we summarized these scales, Ayelet admitted that she was in a 'good position in the middle or maybe a little higher'. As a homework assignment, she was asked to rate her appearance every day as she felt and thought of herself in relation to: (a) the day before, (b) her friends, and (c) her family.

She practiced this method for more than a month, bringing me each continuum at the start of our weekly sessions. We examined and re-examined the questions: 'How do you feel about yourself today in relation to how you used to think and feel about yourself? What other changes would you like to achieve in your feeling? How do you think you can contribute to this change?'

The change in Ayelet's self-evaluation was evident from the changes that evolved in her appearance. When I first met her, she would wear long oversized black sweaters and would tie her hair back very carefully. She continued wearing black; however, her clothes became tighter fitting and shorter, and she began to use colorful accessories such as red ribbons or multicolored vests. She started letting her hair down loose and became more and more beautiful. (A year later, when she started therapy with her boyfriend, she wore shorts, and he told me she was wearing a bikini to the beach!)

At the two-year mark of therapy, Ayelet continued to refuse to look at herself in the mirror or to perform any exercise I suggested relating to a mirror. However, I thought she must get acquainted with her real body. I decided to use Mahoney's (1991) method of mirror working. She agreed to use a very small hand mirror. We began with her looking only at the toes on her left foot. She laughed while doing this, hesitating a little, but, as usual, she tried to do her best. In that session she became able to move the mirror and look over her whole leg. Over the next four weeks, she was asked as homework to look at one additional body part each day and then to demonstrate this to me during the sessions. As she progressed and she was able to look at her body, she could admit she was not that bad looking. However, she was too frightened when it came time for her to look at her face in the mirror. Exploiting her creativity, in the next session I made her prepare masks, color them, and look at herself through the masks. It was a very fun session because she made masks of witches and laughed when she looked at herself. She kept changing masks, from that of a man to that of a woman. Finally she said, 'Well, I wouldn't like to be a man. I want to be a woman. Do you think I will ever be able to have a normal life, have sex and children?'

It was the first time Ayelet had mentioned sex, which had been a taboo subject before. She then began talking about her fears that she would be unable to have children because of her previous medical problems. I realized she could now conceive of herself as a sexual woman, and she was beginning to accept her urges and needs. She was already dating her boyfriend, so being concerned about her sexuality was not any longer generalized anxiety but a specific fear whether or not she could build normal healthy relationships with him. At first, she was very much ashamed of her past history. She expected her boyfriend's family to reject her and get against their relationship. He urged her not to share her past history with people (especially his family) before they learned to know her closely. He trusted that when people got to know her better they would love and respect her. Then they would not be frightened by her past, but learn to respect her coping abilities. He was right. As soon as his family learned to know Ayelet, they started to love her.

The experience with her boyfriend and his family was very important for Ayelet. She learned that she could control her life without being haunted by her past. But this is not something that came immediately or naturally. We had to work and deal with it. Only after a long time as a couple did Ayelet learn that love and trust can be a wonderful change agent, and that she had nothing to be ashamed of or needs to conceal.

14

Incorporating Ayelet's Creativity, Imagination and Talent

Ayelet demonstrated a great creative urge: She wrote poetry and stories, kept lists, painted, and shared her daydreams and nighttime dreams. Around this time, as we worked on her self-acceptance, I decided to tap her creative imagination as a technique for change (Ronen, in press). Lazarus (1984) compared the brain to an extremely intricate and dynamic computer that stores voices, pictures, and images. Each event is transferred into images and thoughts that influence our actions. The brain collects many creative solutions if we are inventive and allow images to arise. Ayelet showed an aptitude for using her creative skills, implying that she had the courage to take risks. I could challenge her during every session to imagine herself coping, progressing, and entering a new world of excitement and experiences (Ronen, in press).

In view of Ayelet's difficulties talking about sensitive issues and the fact that she drew and painted regularly, I asked her to let me into her world through her art. After several sessions of artwork, she arrived one day with a big portfolio of all her pictures from the period of her hospitalizations (see Part I of the book). She put the portfolio down in front of me, saying, 'This is my world of emptiness and nothing. Take it. I don't want it anymore.' All of the drawings were on old parchment-like paper, in black ink. All of them showed human figures, but there were no signs of sexuality. The figures looked like trees, and most seemed – from their long hair – to be of women, always in a gesture of prayer, crying or asking for help.

During that part of treatment, we used many metaphors. Ayelet used to talk about the black hole she was in and about the emptiness she was sensing. I used to ask her to imagine she was in that hole. I wanted her to try describing what it was like to be there. Then, gradually, I asked her to try bringing me inside that hole. Together, we would find ways out of there, find ways to brighten the hole, and discover things with which to fill the emptiness.

I used positive creative imagination to help create a good picture of the future (Ronen, in press). At first, this future had to be 'in 500 years' time' because Ayelet did not believe it was possible. Later, as she became able to imagine some of the good things that could happen 500 years on, we could start making them come true earlier.

I believe that trying to speak in her language – of metaphors, imagery, poetry, drawing, and art – was the main tool that helped me bridge the gap between Ayelet and myself, and between her sickness and health.

15

Couple Therapy

When Ayelet started dating and fell in love, she shared her relationship with her boyfriend with me. As the relationship became serious, she insisted on me seeing her together with her boyfriend. First, she wanted him to know exactly who she was, with no secrets or surprises. Second, she wanted him to know all the possible risks to their future together. Third, she wanted my help in learning to live together, starting to have sex, and overcoming some of her inhibitions and intimacy difficulties. Finally, Ayelet emphasized the fact that since they were serious about each other, she and her boyfriend needed to receive guidance.

Ayelet's boyfriend was the best thing that could ever have happened to her. He adored her yet never gave up his wish for her to change. He asked my advice on ways to help her. He made her change the way she dressed, daring her to put on more attractive clothes. He made her join him in social activities and dance together. He did not fear her rejection of sex and consulted me about how to overcome it.

It is important for me to add that the relationship between Ayelet and her boyfriend did not develop as a fairy tale. It was not as if they felt in love and everything was immediately perfect. However, there was enough basic love and trust to ensure that they would be able to solve these conflicts, and find a way to live together. For example, trying to overcome their sex problems, they worked together on assignments such as standing naked in front of the mirror, looking at themselves while hugging and kissing. He could help her where I could not, and with lots of love and care, he helped her to have sex and enjoy it.

At the time of this writing they are married and living happily together. They are a very loving couple. He works in the military, and she teaches her special education class. Together, they are raising their two young children. After they married, they used to come to me once in a while, mainly for consultation. She is very dependent on him, and eats almost normally in his presence. I still do not trust her eating habits when she is alone. As of now, she eats well for her husband's sake, but I also think that her eating and health habits have changed during pregnancy and will improve still further as a natural result of her desire to be a good mother.

I believe that motherhood is very good for Ayelet. She is a good mother and wife. The pregnancy has made her more calm, relaxed, and accepting. She found it to be a corrective experience, assuaging her concerns about her own femininity and fertility. As far as her maternal capabilities, Ayelet's experiences have taught her to be very sensitive and considerate of others and have given her tools to cope and overcome serious hurdles. Both these aspects should serve her well as a new mother.

16

Interim Summary

Ayelet was in therapy for four years. Over the years of treatment, Ayelet evidenced remarkable changes in all areas of her life. In keeping with the multiple-treatment design, each of her problem areas other than eating disorders and self-acceptance (family, OCD, anxiety and fears, vocational, social skills) did not improve until we started treating it. Then, each improved greatly soon after we started working toward change. Post-treatment self-evaluation revealed significant improvement in comparison to baseline assessment.

Working on familial change improved the quality of relationships between Ayelet and each of her parents, with an increased ability for emotional expression and physical touch. This first area of change was a lasting one that continued improving over the years of treatment. Ayelet was very motivated for change and did her best to comply with therapy, as manifested in the change she evidenced in her OCD, anxieties, and fears. Major progress was also evident in Ayelet's vocational involvement. At first, she was not able to discuss it, make phone calls, or look at the classifieds. Yet, within weeks, she was able to enroll in a course of study. She graduated the four-year bachelor program in special education (with honors), obtained her teaching license, and began working as a teacher in a special education class, which she continues to do to this day.

Ayelet started acquiring social skills while we worked toward fear reduction and exposure tasks, but she felt more secure and ready to communicate with friends later on, as we practiced social skills. An impressive area of change was Ayelet's self-acceptance and self-evaluation, which underwent changes even prior to direct treatment. As we started working on these directly, she became able to compliment herself and admit her own abilities. She turned into a pleasant, happy, nice young woman. Ayelet today appears self-confident and secure. The most striking change in her is the way she stopped perceiving herself as a bad person. She is now able to say that she is a good teacher and a good wife and mother. She even seems to like herself. Ayelet does continue to be very sensitive and perfectionist. She needs to do everything the best possible way, works hard, and cannot accept incompleteness.

As I mentioned above, we never worked directly on Ayelet's eating habits, but these demonstrated improvement while her other problems were in focus. Gradually, as she felt better adjusted in her family, less anxious, more successful vocationally and socially, and more accepting of herself physically and emotionally, Ayelet stopped using laxative medications, stopped vomiting, and started having regular bowel movements. Today, six years later at age 27, she still worries about gaining weight and carefully watches everything she eats. She says that the anorexic thoughts are always on her mind, and she doesn't believe she can get rid of them. However, now she is also certain that she does not want to lose weight or endanger her life. She eats because she has reasons to live a healthy life – a husband, children, work, and family.

I do not know how to end this story. There is no end. It is the story of a struggle that continues every day. But each time there is more hope, and more smiles. I believe that love, trust, and hope are really the most important features in helping Ayelet live with herself and progress.

PART III

Ayelet's Story

Life after Anorexia

I

Feedback

It is strange to think of myself as someone who used to be anorexic. I feel now like somebody standing on one side of the ocean, talking about someone who has been left behind on the distant shore.

Writing this book was a special experience for me. First of all, because it gave me a chance to go back and understand my past better. But also, because I was fortunate enough to be able to become acquainted with all the considerations leading Tammie to treat me the way she had. I saw her, as my therapist during treatment, as a very empathic, creative, smart, sensitive person. Writing this book together enabled me to learn more about her doubts, fears, and uncertainties. I realized that she was not so different from me. We share many of the same kind of feelings and the same kinds of thoughts. But, we behave differently. This made me eager to continue learning, progressing, and working to help others the way she helped me.

While writing this book, Tammie reminded me of many things I did not recall. It is strange how I can remember each word of our discussion as we started couple therapy together with my husband, but how I forgot so many things relating to earlier periods. Maybe this is because I do not like the person I was, and I wish to put behind and forget those periods of my life.

For example, my treatment started with family therapy; yet, I have no memories from those sessions. How can that be the case? Did I dislike these sessions? Were they less significant than other parts of my therapy? Was I embarrassed by all the things we had to talk about in my family?

Several memories relating to my anorexic problems are still very vivid. My parents always insisted that I gain weight and wanted

Tammie to help me start eating. Tammie, on the other hand, backed me up, saying that she was not going to deal with pounds. She said she did not wish for me to gain weight and did not want to be kept occupied by weighing me. She said that what was important for her was that I feel good, be healthy, and try not to lose weight. That was a real starting point for me. Immediately, she recruited my cooperation. I also appreciated the fact that Tammie wanted the two of us to make a treatment contract, considering my wishes and cooperation. Unlike other therapies, it was not Tammie deciding and me needing to comply. Neither was there a coalition between my therapist and my parents against my wishes. Here, for the first time, I would receive a mutual, equal contract. I felt I could trust her and open up to her.

I was happy with the way Tammie demanded that my parents let go of me, refrain from interfering, and allow me to be responsible for the treatment. For the first time, I felt that maybe I was a grown-up person who could even perhaps be trusted.

I was also fascinated by the fact that I received Tammie's permission to call her between sessions and talk with her whenever I felt the need. Treatment was not as formal as I was accustomed to, e.g. me talking, and the therapist listening. We were talking together, sometimes joking or laughing, sometimes even crying together. I felt I had a partner with me, not against me.

I was faced with a new kind of relationship, with which I was unfamiliar. For the first time, I started feeling that maybe there were hope, optimism, and good things waiting for me in the future.

By accepting my thoughts and emotions, through a long process, the change has occurred.

Finally, I found myself accepting different behaviors, different ways of thinking and feeling and believing. I cannot tell exactly when it happened. It was a very slow, gradual process of acceptance. Tammie helped me achieve our goals in the treatment by learning to know who I was, learning my kind of language, and becoming part of my belief system. Only then could she help me change and choose another way to live.

2

And What Now? And What Next?

During the last few months, and especially as an outcome of writing this book, I keep asking myself: So, who am I? What has really changed? Did I really change? How can it be that I am married and have a husband and two children and a good job? Am I different?

We were looking at my drawings from the past, of very pessimistic, black, thin, asexual figures. Tammie asked whether I had any recent drawings and writings. After being released from the last hospital, I had stopped writing and drawing. But, as I started my studies for special education, we had art lessons, and I was asked to write and draw again. I searched through my old notebooks and found some assignments I had done. When I compared these with the old drawings and writings , I found both similarities and changes. I was amazed by both, and the comparison helped me learn more about myself, my way of thinking, and my way of interpreting the world.

First of all, the most notable change is the kind of paper I used. At the hospital, I used to write on small pages of yellow, imitation old paper. The new pictures I drew were on big sheets of white paper. Also, the new drawings were no longer limited to black pen, but rather were colorful with a variety of shades and hues. I even used colors that could be spread around and were not as controllable as the pen I used before. Tammie said that colors indicate the variety of emotion one is able to express, and that erasing and using only pen or crayon might attest to anxiety and a need for control. So, I am no longer that anxious person I was; I can show a larger range of emotion; and I can allow myself to give up control sometimes.

It was interesting to see that the motive of water that had been part of many of my drawings in the past also appeared in the later drawings, but differently. In the past, I used to draw tears, symbols of pain and agony. In the later drawings, I drew running water. The water symbolized life, fertility, and happiness. One of my more recent pictures, *Drops of Water* (illustration 21), depicted a faucet and drops of water coming out of it. It was colored in brown, blue, and yellow.

Looking at this picture, it seems obvious that a faucet is something that can be turned off and turned on; that is, it can be controlled. Under this drawing I had written:

Water in the glass, water in the sea, water in the swimming pool
Water running, water in the faucet
Dark water, pure water
Sweet water, bitter water
Warm water, cold water
A drop of water
An endless amount of water
Water, water all day long
Water for the whole world
My water, your water
The water of and for all
Your hand will be the one to decide
What kind of water it will be
You, me, maybe someone else
I am different, I have changed
But I am still me

Another recent drawing, *Watering the Earth* (illustration 22), was of a human figure. Again, it was drawn on a large sheet of white paper. The person was watering the ground. It is very obvious that in contrast with the past, the dark sad past, this drawing was very optimistic. The human figure wanted things to grow and therefore watered them. Also, this was the first figure showing some visible, distinct sexual signs, albeit male. At the age of 22, after three years in therapy with Tammie, I still had not drawn a sexual woman. Yet this man represented me. His watering figure was a symbol of strength, using the water to break the underlying rock. Again, I depicted a

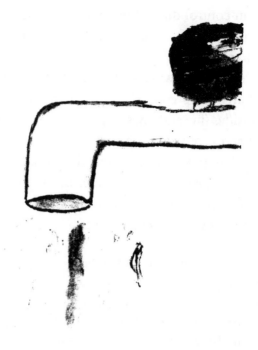

Illustration 21 Drops of Water

Illustration 22 Watering the Earth

person who can control difficulties and overcome them. In all those more recent pictures, difficulties exist, but strengths are also present and can be controlled.

The third item I found was a sculpture I made during my studies. It was a piece of artwork presenting both the inside and the outside. In the past, my insides (me and my soul) were something black, terrible, and painful, whereas outwards I presented an external world that was good and pure. This piece shows a great deal of strength on the inside as well as on the outside. It is no longer black, but rather bright. It portrays lots of hope and faith. As I had to hand in this assignment, I also wrote something that went with it:

> *There is outside, but there is also inside*
> *There is everything*
> *And I have eyes to look and see, and if need be, even glasses*
> *And I have ears to hear and listen, and if need be, even hearing aids*
> *And I have hands, and legs to touch and feel and sense*
> *And I have a heart to love*
> *And I have someone to love*
> *And he also has an inside and an outside*
> *And I chose him*
> *And he is mine*

The writing piece accentuates the integration I was able to create. Bitter and sweet, ugly and beautiful. Accepting all the variety of emotion and behavior. In the past, things for me were black and white. Now, everything is colored. Everything has it own place.

One main issue that has certainly changed is my priorities. Food is not my main concern any longer. It is not that I don't want to be thin. Neither do I mean that I don't hesitate when served food or when I need to eat in front of other people. Food was, and still is, a problem. In fact, I believe that I will always have these anorexic thoughts about the need to be thin. However, while in the past these occupied my mind and comprised the main issue in my life, now they are pushed aside. There are many other, more important things to be busy with and think of. For example, during my pregnancy, I learned to identify the feeling of hunger and realized it was important for me to eat for the baby's sake. While in the past I used to ignore such feelings and push them away, now I did the opposite. I tried to identify the sense of hunger and eat while feeling it. Tammie helped me accept that I didn't have to eat a lot. I never needed to overeat to the point of feeling too full. But I did need to eat something in order to keep healthy and take care of myself and my baby. So I ate a little bit, kept feeling good about it, and was proud of my ability to behave maturely. Because I didn't eat too much, I didn't have those terrible feelings of self-blame or physical pain. So, I learned to eat. A little, but enough to stay alive and healthy.

Another thing I learned through therapy was the different roles played by food in my life. I learned to stop using food when I wanted to express something (mainly, to fight with my parents). It stopped being my way of assessing my own self-acceptance. So many times in the past I ate, or did not eat, because of different kinds of emotions unrelated to the need for food. Now, I am trying to deal with the emotions themselves, and I certainly do not do so by using food. Thus, food has no emotional role anymore. Food is food. It has returned to its rightful place. Eating or dieting is no longer a substitute for any kind of emotion. It is something you do to stay alive, to be healthy, or sometimes just to enjoy it.

Talking about comprehending food's rightful place, I think there were several factors that helped me reach that point. One was working on my emotions, self-acceptance, and self-confidence during therapy. Another was the fact that my relationships with my parents had changed, and food was no longer an issue in my family. Yet, a main factor affecting this change was related to my husband (who was my boyfriend at the time) – the way he helped me learn to eat again. Tammie used to say that my boyfriend was her change agent and that he was her main helper. They used to exchange smiles when she said things, and my then boyfriend proudly would turn to me, and say: 'You see? I told you!!!'

My husband first of all accepted me as I was, with my problems. And despite all that, he kept thinking that I was wonderful. I used to talk about my problems, and he used to talk about how beautiful, smart, and sensitive I was. So, slowly, I began looking at myself with his eyes, trying to find the whole me, this wonderful personality who had impressed him. The exercises in front of the mirror, me alone and the two of us together, also helped.

From the start and up to this day, my husband and I share food and share plates. We eat together. We don't have his plate or her plate, but, rather, our plate. In the beginning, eating from the same plate, as something that combined us, that we shared together, made eating easier for me.

I guess some health problems will always remain with me. I often suffer from all kinds of stomach aches, suffer from constipation, and sometimes vomit. Expecting all these problems to disappear magically, as if they never were, is only a dream. But, after fearing that I would never be able to get pregnant or have a child, I am deeply thankful for the fact that I could have that, and have a normal life. In contrast to the kind of pain I would have endured if I were childless, these pains have simply become something I learned to live with and accept. In the past, I used to wish it would all disappear, and I would work toward overcoming it. However, another thing I learned in therapy was that there are some things you can overcome, but there are many you have to learn to accept and live with. Accepting this physical discomfort as part of me transformed it into a reminder of what I had done to myself. A memory I will always have to live with, but at the same time, something I can withstand while continuing to conduct a normal life.

The experience of anorexia taught me an important lesson about my body's needs. I used to fill myself with so many unneeded medications: to vomit, empty myself, and lose weight. Now I no longer use any such medications, and I believe that it is important to watch what foreign substances I ingest.

I do sometimes have flashbacks to the awful places I used to be in, as if some old movie is running, reminding me of the past. But if I do find myself close to those places, and I get frightened, I take care to return very quickly, knowing that I don't need a shelter any longer. I have nothing to hide.

Looking at the concept of hiding is very important. I used to see myself as a bad person who deserved punishment. I used to try hiding all the garbage inside me. That garbage has disappeared completely. I know I am a good person. I'm not always satisfied with the way I behave. I always think I can do better. But I do believe that I am good, that I deserve to live. I know I am important to my environment. And the most important thing, I don't hide. I deal with disturbing issues. I talk about them. I don't try to hide things or ignore them. I know how important it is to deal with emotions, as difficult as they are.

It is hard to understand that anorexic girls do not have misconceptions relating to other people or to the world, but only misconceptions relating to themselves. This distortion is strange and difficult to accept. How can a girl relate so gently to everyone else but not to herself? I don't have the explanation, but I know this is what happened with me as well as with many other anorexic girls.

The process of change is very tricky and difficult. On the one hand, accepting and understanding was very important. On the other hand, if I had not been pushed toward change, acceptance alone would never have sufficed. I would have stayed the same. So, what really helped me was the combination of demanding, urging, and pushing, together with empathy and understanding. And most of all love, belief, and fantasies of a better future. It was only once I could dream of living better and could envision myself enjoying life that I was able to start working toward change.

And lastly (this time, really my last remark), as difficult as anorexia is, as low as the rate of success is, there is always hope. One can be changed. It is possible to overcome, change, and cope. It is possible to learn to enjoy life. Hope is the most important thing of all. The path into anorexia is extremely difficult, but there is always a way out.

PART IV

Literature Review

In this part of the book, I will review the pertinent literature on Ayelet's illness, on the anorexia disorder and its treatment. In addition, I will provide a theoretical framework for the cognitive-constructivist intervention that I applied in treating Ayelet. I will include the basics of cognitive therapy and of constructivist therapy, and the treatment process for cognitive-constructivist therapy in general and for children and adolescents in particular. Finally, I will review self-control therapy for children. I will describe in detail the theoretical and practical guidelines underlying the self-control model that I developed, which I implemented in Ayelet's treatment.

I

The Anorexia Disorder

Anorexia nervosa is classified in the literature either as an eating disorder (along with bulimia, Foreyt and McGavin 1988) or as a somatic disorder (Siegel and Smith 1991). The medico-clinical approach defines the illness in terms of its clinical manifestations; that is, the presence of some central features necessary for the diagnostic criteria (Russell 1995). Its main feature is the restriction of eating (Theander 1995). The DSM-IV (American Psychiatric Association 1994) defines anorexia as a refusal to maintain body weight over a minimal normal weight for age and height, with a loss of 15 percent below expected body weight. An intense fear of gaining weight or becoming fat is experienced, as well as disturbances in perceptions of body size, weight, or shape. In girls who already have their period, at least three consecutive menstrual cycles are absent.

The disorder is typically associated with serious electrolyte imbalances and other medical abnormalities (Palla and Litt 1988). It appears that the multiple physiological disturbances are the result of the weight loss and caloric restriction, rather than the cause of the disorder. Anorexia can pose grave danger to the client, with estimated mortality as high as 15 percent (Dally 1969; Palla and Litt 1988). However, clients may fully recover, including those who were very ill (Theander 1995). Almost all women diet during their adolescent or early adult years. However, very few go on to develop anorexia. The mechanism that triggers this development is still unknown (Halmi 1995). According to the medico-clinical approach, there is increasing evidence of biological vulnerability in terms of susceptibility to disregulation or dysfunction of the neurotransmitter systems that regulate eating behavior as well as emotion (Halmi 1995).

In contrast, the sociocultural approach to causation views the disorder as a response to prevailing social and cultural systems (Russell 1995). Modern societal pressures may be responsible for determining the nature of our clients' preoccupations, which are held obstinately and amount to over-valued ideas (Russell 1995). The disorder has undergone major changes over the years, in congruence with societal attitudes attributing great importance to female thinness. The psychological content of anorexia has evolved from the wish to lose weight into clients' expression of a dread of fatness. The strong environmental influence has been linked to the widespread emphasis in the media on the importance of looking good and being thin, with its focus on the female body. For example, it has been suggested that there is a higher frequency of anorexia in an athletic environment (Thompson and Sherman 1999), and among fashion models, actresses, and dancers.

Anorexia has become more frequent over the last several decades, mostly among the middle and upper socioeconomic classes. It characterizes mainly adolescents (12 to 22 years old), with a higher frequency of girls in comparison with boys. Yet, recently, increasing numbers of boys with anorexia are being reported. Bulimia nervosa has appeared as a new variant of anorexia nervosa, and has already exceeded anorexia in scope.

As can be seen, all of the above features were present in Ayelet's anorexia. Ayelet was 14 years old when she began dieting. She lost over 33 pounds (about 25% of her body weight), she lost her period, and she feared gaining weight.

Anorexia nervosa is a complex disorder (Foreyt and McGavin 1988). Its complexity has been related to three major issues. One concerns the people involved in the disorder's development and maintenance. Anorexia involves not only the individual, but also the family and the wider environment. There is, therefore, a need to address all of these during assessment and treatment planning. The second issue relates to the behavioral, emotional, and cognitive components that influence each of the involved parties. In other words, anorexia comprises a disorder relating to all major components of the person's functioning, rather than a problem caused by one main factor such as only the person's dysfunctional behavior. Third, anorexia constitutes an umbrella disorder that encompasses diverse elements such as obsessions, poor self-image and self-acceptance, anxiety and fears, social skill deficits, cognitive skill deficits, etc. Each of these requires attention and, often, different approaches.

Thus, the complexity of the anorexia disorder has led to the development of various assessment and intervention models that offer different explanations, definitions of normality, and suggestions regarding what and how change needs to be implemented. One can refer to anorexia using a metaphor of three blind people, who each possess knowledge of a different part of an elephant and who argue as to what an elephant is. Perhaps the only constant factor in this ever-changing, complex syndrome of anorexia nervosa (and its sister, bulimia nervosa) is that its victims are invariably psychiatrically vulnerable young women (Silverman 1995).

One of the difficulties in assessing anorexia derives from the large population of women who are constantly occupied with their appearance, dieting, irresponsible eating habits, and disturbances in self-acceptance. However, psychological studies have suggested that, as a group, anorexics tend to be perfectionists, to feel personally ineffective, to exhibit interpersonal distrust, and to lack awareness or exhibit confusion over internal emotional and physiological states (Bruch 1973, 1977; Strober 1980). These features of anorexic females were all shown to be less common among normal dieting females (Garner 1986).

Ayelet could be a perfect model for the above description. Her illness was complex, involving family members and typified by complex relationships with them. It was also linked with her social relationships. Yet, most of all, Ayelet was a perfectionist, obsessed, anxious person, who had always been occupied with herself, her emotions, and her position in the world in which she lived.

2

Treatment of Anorexia

During the last decade, many theories, techniques, and interventions have been applied to anorexia. Yet the disorder remains a challenge in terms of understanding and treatment (Fairburn, Shafran and Cooper 1999). Anorexia continues to be seen by clinicians as one of the most frustrating and recalcitrant forms of psychopathology.

The complexity of treatment for anorexic youngsters is closely linked to the characteristics of teenagers having the disorder. One difficulty stems from anorexic clients' typical reluctance to seek and comply with treatment. They demonstrate a tendency to misinterpret and a strong ambivalence toward therapeutic intervention (Schmidt 1998; Ward et al. 1996; Williamson et al. 1999). This reluctance to commit to treatment is accompanied by these youngsters' intense resistance to change, highlighting the crucial importance of establishing the client–therapist relationship.

Other features contributing to the difficulty in treating anorexic clients relate to their biased information processing and their denial of the danger inherent in their eating habits. Treatment thus also necessitates collaboration between physician and therapist. The need to control weight loss and eating habits often leads to the implementation of treatment in a hospital or institution-based setting. Often treatment must be recurrent and prolonged (Freeman 1995).

Anorexia is treated differently in accordance with various theoretical approaches. There have been four major models in treating anorexia: biological, psychodynamic, family, and cognitive-behavioral orientations. I will briefly relate to the first three, and then will focus on the treatment I used with Ayelet, the cognitive-constructivist approach.

The Biological Model

Research into the biological aspects of eating disorders has examined the effects of dieting on neurobiology and neuroendocrine systems, in addition to identifying biological abnormalities in clients with eating disorders (Wilson, Heffernan and Black 1996). As eating behavior can affect changes in neurobiology and vice versa, the research in this area is very complex. However, it is agreed that there are three possible etiologies for anorexia: the hormonal changes that occur at puberty, the relationship between depression and eating disorders, and brain functioning. Therefore, treatment consists of medication to change mood, emotion, and brain function and to induce homeostasis of hormones (Foreyt and McGavin 1988).

The Psychodynamic Model

The psychodynamic approach views anorexia as a syndrome of unconscious, internal conflicts that stem from early development. These conflicts involve sexuality, autonomy, and identity. Food intake might be linked, for example, to pregnancy fantasies, where the refusal of food serves as a defense against an infantile fantasy of oral impregnation by the father (Bruch 1973, 1986). Crisp (1980) has described anorexics as having a 'weight phobia' that results from fears of maturation and sexuality. The focus according to this approach is not on food intake itself, but rather on the motives and emotions underlying the disorder.

The psychoanalytic treatment of anorexia is directed toward facilitating the development of an understanding of the meaning of the client's communications, symptoms, and emotional life. It focuses on an attempt to find meaning in the client's symptoms. Psychoanalytic thinking submits the idea that the somatic state can provide a symbolic picture of trauma (Dare and Crowther 1995). Vomiting, for example, has been understood as an attempt to eliminate an unwanted penis from an oral sexual trauma. Fear of fatness may be a rejection of any possible pregnancy. Thinness may symbolize actual fear, and starvation may consist of a symbolic way to express aggression (Dare and Crowther 1995).

Another important aspect of anorexia nervosa within the psychodynamic approach consists of the aggressive drive, which is viewed as a derivative of the death wish. Dare and Crowther (1995) stated that anorexic clients are so controlled, in so much of their lives, that they become 'screaming, scraggy bundles of fury in defense of their right to starve'. Whereas the client does not allow herself to directly express anger and to enact frustration and rage, self-starvation is viewed as a legitimate way to express aggression. Another aspect addressed by psychodynamic therapy is the fact that anorexic clients fear the vulnerability of closeness. Anorexia is thus viewed as a symptom enabling clients to avoid close relationships and to gain back control over their lives.

Psychodynamic therapy, therefore, is a process that helps the client to become aware of and understand their internal emotional processes, drives, and motives; release their fears; and gain insight into their need to use such complex symptoms. An important therapeutic feature is the mutual acceptance of the nature of the joint work and the alliance created between client and therapist. The therapist tries to establish an atmosphere of trust and empathy and to formulate the focal hypothesis (Dare and Crowther 1995). Therapy targets thoughts and feelings that are not openly expressed but rather are guessed to be somewhere in the client's mind (Dare and Crowther 1995). Clients are invited to look into their own minds in order to understand unconscious difficulties. Then, clients are expected to self-analyze their symptoms, their internalized representations of the significant people in their lives, and their relationships with them. This process is conducted via evolving patterns of feelings between the client and the therapists, which create the transference/counter-transference relationships. Clients are taught about the function of their symptoms in order to be able to release them, and are encouraged to replace the difficult symptoms with different, more adaptive behavior (Dare and Crowther 1995).

The Family Model

Family therapy focuses on the complex family social system, in which the various family features are seen as part of a complex matrix of interacting factors (Eisler 1995). Family patterns are considered to render an important contribution to the anorexia disorder (Dare and Key 1999; Gowers and North 1999). These patterns include features such as over-protectiveness, enmeshment, inability to express and resolve conflict openly, detachment, and lack of empathy and affection (Minuchin *et al.* 1975; Minuchin, Rossman and Baker 1978). Gowers and North (1999) investigated the relationship between severity of anorexia nervosa and difficulties in family functioning. They suggested a list of family features that impact on family functioning and contribute to the development of eating disorders, including parental disharmony, parental eating disorders, abuse, and sibling delinquency. Bruch (1973) claimed that the heart of anorexia nervosa lies in particular early mother–child relationships, in which appropriate maternal responses to the child's needs are lacking. Instead, the mother acts on her own need to feel in control. Most studies have reported a lower level of perceived closeness or, at least, a level of closeness lower than the respondent would really like. Communication in general, and emotional expression in particular, has been reported as restricted in many studies (Eisler 1995). Although family factors contribute to the development of eating disorders, no particular type of family constellation or style of family functioning has been invariably associated with eating disorders (Eisler 1995).

In family therapy, interventions focus on the identifying of the roles and communication within the family; the establishment of age-appropriate hierarchical organization and boundaries within the family; the encouragement of a clear alliance between the adults of the family for the sake of effective parenting; and the exploration of the history of the family in order to identify the family members' specific traditions, attitudes, and expectations from family life (Dare and Eisler 1995).

Family therapy defines which part of treatment comprises sessions with the parents only, and which part targets the family as a unit. Emphasis is placed on the role that the client's illness has come to play in the pattern of family life. The therapist tries to help the family members modify those patterns that seem to diminish their capacity to be effective in challenging and restructuring the client's eating habits and that tend to perpetuate the client in a sick role that differs from her siblings' roles (Dare and Eiser 1995). Therapy focuses on changing roles, relationships, and communication styles within the family.

The Cognitive-Behavioral Model

Traditionally, most anorexic clients have been treated using behavioral models. With the increase of cognitive theories, behavioral therapy has evolved into cognitive-behavioral therapy (CBT). Over the last decade, another shift has incorporated the constructivist components. For the purpose of clarity, considering that this comprises my main intervention model, I will first discuss the main components of each theory separately – behavioral, cognitive, and constructivist – and then I will focus on the combination of the three.

Behavior therapy

Behavioral theory and therapy focus on learning methods. Highlighting the link between behavior and its consequences, behavior is analyzed by its outcome. When a behavior is followed by a positive outcome for the client, it will continue. The behavioral literature views anorexia as a conditional avoidance response to real or perceived fears related to weight, development, and performance (Garner 1986). Behavioral treatment methods therefore focus mainly on desensitization and exposure techniques to decrease the fear of weight gain (Garner 1986). Treatment directs clients to increase their weight by controlling factors associated with maladaptive patterns, with an emphasis on weight gain, cessation of vomiting, and the design of appropriate eating habits. Environmental contingencies are applied to establish a minimal acceptable weight. Hospitalized clients must gain weight in order to receive permission to leave the hospital for a short while, visit their families, or obtain other rewards.

Other environmental contingency methods are directed toward the maximization of caloric intake, food consumption, and weight gain by making activities, privileges, and reinforcements contingent upon eating behavior (Siegel and Smith 1991). According to this behavioral approach, only after resolving the primary health care problem of eating can attention be shifted to other issues such as misconceptions, fears, and emotions.

Anorexia has also been widely treated by additional behavioral techniques such as the application of systematic desensitization for decreasing fears of being fat, operant reinforcement combining reinforcement programs with family therapy, and the use of physical activity as a reinforcement for weight gain. The latter is based on the premark principle, e.g. the observation that many anorexic clients exhibit a high level of activity.

A derivative of both family and behavioral models has also been applied to anorexia, the behavioral family systems therapeutic approach (Robin and Siegel 1999). This approach highlights the role of each member of the family on the development and maintenance of the disorder, mobilizing the family members' support for change and for increasing the efficacy of treatment.

Debates abound concerning the efficacy of behavioral therapy for the anorexic population. Behavioral methods have been found effective in achieving weight gain; however, Bruch (1986) argued that such methods alone can result in further psychological damage if not incorporated into treatment of other issues.

Cognitive therapy

Cognitive theory and therapy view behavior as an outcome of the link between thoughts and emotions. Therapy is focused on clarifying this link. Cognitive theories view cognitive components as responsible for the occurrence of anorexia. Central to cognitive theory is the hypothesis that beliefs and expectancies pertaining to body size and to eating are biased in favor of selectively processed information relating to thinness, dieting, and control of food intake or body weight (Williamson *et al.* 1999).

The cognitive component of treatment provides an important complement to behavioral components. Cognitive treatments emphasize the functional correlations between antecedents, consequences, and individual behaviors in order to understand the anorexic youngster's misperceptions regarding self-concept, separation, perfectionism, and relationships. According to this approach, cognitions are considered the most important links in the chain of events leading from thoughts and emotions to behaviors (Powell and Oei 1991).

Cognitive therapeutic techniques include: cognitive structuring to modify misconceptions; problem analysis to emphasize the link between the event, the thought, and the behavior; attentional focus to increase awareness of internal stimuli; and self-control practice to acquire skills for overcoming and changing behavior (Ronen and Rosenbaum 1998; Rosenbaum and Ronen 1998). The aim of therapy is for the client to gradually acquire the ability to better respond to challenging environmental pressures (Guidano 1995).

Fairburn *et al.* (1999) proposed a cognitive explanation for anorexia nervosa based on the client's need for control. Suggesting a control-based therapeutic approach, they recommended self-control training to maintain eating, shape, and weight, as well as to meet the client's general need for control.

Constructivist therapy

Constructivist theory and therapy emphasize the personal meaning-making process. That is, human beings are seen as responsible for the idiosyncratic way in which they construct and construe their own behaviors, thoughts, and emotions. These constructs allow people to interpret, predict, and appropriately respond to their subsequent experiences (Neimeyer 1995). Personal constructions are responsible for the individual's knowledge of self and the world, which regulates perceptions of environmental events and may contribute to maladaptive perceptions (Guidano 1995). Of particular focus are cognitive structures relating to personal identity (Guidano and Liotti 1983) and the role of information processing, self-representation, personality variables, and motivation (Vitousek and Hollon 1990). The way human beings construct their lives is strongly influenced by their expectancies and beliefs, and the meaning-making process is continuously influenced by the interactions between thought, emotion, and behavior. For example, anorexic clients' distortions in self-image, such as 'I hate my body', 'Nobody will like me if I'm fat', and 'Only thin girls succeed in life/are happy', represent their way of constructing and construing events. These personal constructions, rather than reality, will cause their lives and distress to be seen as they are. Therefore, self-organization of experiences encompasses an important concept in constructivist theory (Mahoney 1995). Constructivist treatments emphasize the need to understand the client's particular constructs and to give meaning to the problems they present. Treatment focuses on challenging clients to be open to new experiences, perform exercises, explore new sensations, and experience new techniques for helping people change and improving the quality of their lives.

Currently, no one technique or method appears sufficient to solely resolve the complex difficulties comprising the anorexia disorder. There remains a need to design a comprehensive multi-model treatment approach that relates to the particular set of dysfunctional features presented by the specific client. An integration of techniques and approaches to anorexia has been suggested in the present book. Owing to the fact that cognitive-constructivist therapy comprises the basic theoretical foundation that I espouse in this book, in the next section I will elaborate more fully on this integrated approach's theory, therapy, and techniques.

3

Cognitive-Constructivist Intervention

My treatment of Ayelet combined cognitive and constructivist therapies. I will, therefore, in this chapter, first review the basics of cognitive therapy and then the basics of constructivist therapy, followed by a presentation of the integrated cognitive-constructivist treatment approach in general and as specifically applied to children and adolescents.

The Basics of Cognitive Therapy

A major principle in cognitive theory consists of the view of clients as active participants in their own learning and change processes. Human behavior is seen as being in a constant process of change; therefore, people are always able to render changes in their behavior. Relating to change, the same rule explaining normal human behavior can explain deviations. As a scientific approach, cognitive therapy relies on empirical studies of human behavior based on the results of behavioral assessment and constant evaluation (Hersen and Bellack 1981). An important emphasis is on the interaction between behavior and environment, whereby change can be achieved by modifying either the environment or the individual.

Thinking is considered to play an important role in the etiology and maintenance of disorders (Alford and Beck 1997; Hollon and Beck 1994). Cognitive theories are based on the belief that cognitive mediational processes are involved in human learning. A person's thoughts, images, perceptions, and other cognitive mediating events are presumed to affect behavior. Thoughts, feelings, and behaviors are causally interrelated and affect human relationships.

The task of the cognitive-behavioral therapist is to collaborate with the client to assess distorted or deficient cognitive processes and behaviors and to design new learning experiences that may remediate the dysfunctional or deficient cognitions, behaviors, and emotional patterns. Cognitive therapy is a purposeful attempt to incorporate the cognitive activities of the client within the effort to produce therapeutic change (Kendall and Hollon 1979).

The underlying theoretical rationale for cognitive and constructivist therapy is that an individual's emotions and behavior are largely determined by the way in which he or she structures the world (Beck 1963, 1976; Beck, Emery and Greenberg 1985). A person's cognitions (verbal or pictorial 'events' in the stream of consciousness) are based on attitudes or assumptions (schemata) developed from previous experiences (Beck *et al.* 1990). Cognitions are considered the most important links in the chain of events leading to disordered behavior and psychological dysfunction (Powell and Oei 1991).

A unique feature of cognitive therapy constitutes its adaptability to the individual characteristics of each human being. No single 'proper' technique or intervention can change human functioning. Rather, cognitive theory highlights the need to design a specific intervention adapted to the specific needs of each individual client. Cognitive therapy constitutes an holistic way of life, a way of thinking and perceiving human functioning and needs, and a way of operating within the environment in order to achieve the most effective means for accomplishing one's aims for a particular client.

The Basics of Constructivist Therapy

During the last two decades, cognitive therapy brought constructivist motifs and features into greater focus. Constructivism, as the latest development in cognitive theory, views the person as a combination of scientist and architect (Kelly 1955). Human beings behave as personal scientists by continually creating conceptual templates from experiences (Kanfer and Schefft 1988; Kelly 1955; Neimeyer and

Mahoney 1995). As scientists, people organize their experiences in a way that creates meaning in their lives. Knowledge comprises the main way in which human beings regulate their perceptions of environmental events (Guidano 1995). Knowledge about both similarities and contrasts can be elicited by the individual's continuous comparison and organization of ongoing life experiences. This knowledge is a chief component in the person's ability (as a scientist) to organize, make sense, and give meaning to life experiences, the self, and the world. Knowledge is progressively shaped and changed in response to challenging environmental pressures (Guidano 1995).

Constructivism emphasizes that each person is responsible for the individual way he or she organizes the way life is lived. Viewing people as architects highlights their role in construing their own world and in constructing a personal reality, via a personal meaning-making process (Kelly 1955; Mahoney 1991, 1995). One's construction system varies and changes as one successively anticipates events and construes their replications. The concept of the meaning-making process is based on the understanding that psychological problems are in large part determined by the way people construe their experiences (Kelly 1955). Viewing each individual as a unique architect, the personal construct intervention advocates first attempting to understand the client and then creating an intervention appropriate for that one human being (Swell 1996).

The way in which that particular individual understands feelings is of paramount importance. According to the constructivist approach, emotion does not exist as an entity separate from cognition and vice versa (Neimeyer 1995; Swell 1996). Emotions are inseparable from the cognitions that play a central role in behavior, and both constitute main components in change processes (Swell 1996).

Change processes in therapy derive from attempts to convert irrational, automatic, or maladaptive emergent core schemata into more rational, mediated, or adaptive beliefs and thought processes. During treatment, changes are regulated and modeled step by step, and maintenance processes are aimed at preserving the functional continuity and sense of oneness inherent in selfhood structures (Guidano 1995). Human change processes are characterized by an oscillating and uncertain pattern, both in their path and in their timing from one step to the next (Mahoney 1991).

Cognitive-Constructivist Treatment Process

Cognitive-constructivist therapy is based on working toward an understanding of the client and then intervening in how that client anticipates experiences (Swell 1996) by creating an intervention appropriate for that one human being. Therapy focuses on the *person*, rather than on the pathological response, and its main purpose is to help people cope better with their lives. This therapeutic approach comprises a very careful, continuous assessment process that attempts to analyze the particular client's needs, existing knowledge about the specific problem, and the client's skills and abilities, in order to determine the treatment of choice. The same problem could be treated differently as a result of decision making related to personal, environmental, and behavioral considerations. Intervention methods vary and can include verbal as well as experiential techniques.

Cognitive-constructivist therapists regularly use a large variety of techniques that constitute what may be termed the method's applied science or art form (Bugental 1987). Joyce (1980) viewed the appropriate use of techniques as a ritualized method of human relatedness and communication or as a stylized language for expressing and exploring the ongoing narrative of life processes. Cognitive-constructivist therapists introduce not only verbal but also nonverbal techniques.

Kanfer and Schefft (1988) proposed six thinking rules to direct the therapist in conducting treatment:

1. *Think behavior.* Often, therapists think problems. They concentrate on the client's problem, making assumptions and interpretations regarding its causes. This rule proposes that the therapist should think about the client's behavior and not the client's problems. Actions rather than problems are the main

dimension on which interchanges in therapy are focused. Ayelet mentioned this while referring to the fact that most therapists related to their diagnosis or to her sickness, and not to what she thought or felt.

2. *Think solution*: Most often, therapists devote more time to thinking of difficulties and problems than to finding solutions. A full problem description requires knowledge not only of the current situation or state but also of a more desirable future, and some indication of how to achieve it. The focus of Ayelet's hospitalizations had not been on what could solve her problems, but rather on how to avoid her death.

3. *Think positive*: Just as therapists help the client to think positively and to focus on small changes and positive forces rather than on difficulties, they must themselves also aspire to positive thinking and reinforce positive outcomes. Ayelet was such a creative, talented girl, and focusing on her positive behavior helped me facilitate the change process.

4. *Think small steps*: Although clients are usually interested in the major, significant changes in their lives, extreme changes are difficult to obtain. Targeting small gradual changes reduces fears, motivates clients, and helps therapists observe and pinpoint difficulties. An accumulation of many small changes constitutes one final, large, and significant change. Breaking up Ayelet's problems into small steps enabled us to focus on one small behavior each time, without frightening her.

5. *Think flexible*: This rule challenges therapists to be creative, modify their traditional interventions, and try to adapt themselves to the client's needs. Gambrill (1990) suggested that therapists: look for disconfirming evidence (which points to alternatives), try to understand other people's points of view (instead of being convinced by your own), use language carefully, watch out for vivid data, move beyond the illusion of understanding, complement clear thinking skills with knowledge, and ask about accuracy. Flexibility in applying

different kinds of treatment methods (creative, nonverbal, etc.) suited Ayelet's nature, instead of just focusing on treatment to make her gain weight.

6. *Think future:* Many therapeutic approaches focus on the past and its role on the client's present. Cognitive therapy challenges therapists to think toward the future, predicting how their client will cope and how they themselves would like to be different or better in the future. The whole process of therapy with Ayelet focused on what she wanted to be in the future, instead of what she did in the past or how she was behaving in the present. This future-focus helped instill new expectancies and beliefs in her ability.

Rosenbaum and Ronen (1998) proposed seven crucial features in combining and applying cognitive and constructivist therapies. The first, as described above, consists of the meaning-making process. The goal of therapy is to help clients develop a new and more suitable way of understanding and accepting the way they behave. The intervention process, therefore, is directed toward understanding the meanings attributed to the client's life, or the meaning of specific events in the person's life. It involves accepting one's own reality and how one processes this reality, as well as trying to adapt the meaning to one's needs. Throughout the whole treatment, I tried to understand what her various behaviors, problems, and needs meant for Ayelet, focusing on how she conceptualized them rather than on my own interpretations of these situations.

The second feature constitutes the systematic and goal directed nature of cognitive-constructivist therapy (Rosenbaum and Ronen 1998). Treatment is planned and executed, and the therapeutic hour is constructed (Beck 1976) with an emphasis on the need to define problems, goals, expectations, means to achieve these goals, assessment, and evaluation of the process. As I presented in Part II, each session with Ayelet was constructed, enabling her to know what we were going to focus on and what was the goal of the session.

The third feature comprises practicing and experiencing. Cognitive-constructivist therapy is not a talking therapy but rather a doing therapy that encompasses practicing and experiencing as central components. Interventions vary and can be verbal or nonverbal, using experiential methods such as role assignments, imagery training, metaphors, writing methods, etc. (Mahoney 1991). Neimeyer (1995) proposed that indirect techniques have an invitational quality, encouraging the client to cultivate the personal poetic sensitivities needed to 'speak into being' whole new worlds of possibility (Mair 1988, p.134). Such methods therefore accentuate the clients' own role in formulating their specific life purposes. The proposed indirect techniques aim to demonstrate problematic areas, clarify processes, and illustrate ways to modify interventions with clients. The techniques can be directed toward each of the seven major cognitive-behavioral therapeutic features, emphasizing any specific feature that is in focus during a particular session. Ayelet practiced constantly both in the session and at home. She practiced and experienced more than she was asked to do, and therefore improved her skills quickly.

The fourth feature involves therapy as a collaborative effort (Beck 1976). Therapist and client are expected to enter into an alliance and to collaborate on joint work in order to achieve the goals of therapy. As I described, the agreement between Ayelet and me, as well as the good relationship and working alliance we established, were crucial for the success of the treatment.

The fifth feature, therapy as a person-focused process, suggests that cognitive-constructivist intervention should aim at treating the person, rather than treating the problem. This view of the person as a whole, which concentrates on the client's feelings, thoughts, and way of living, not only on the client's problem, provides a window into seeing the client's strengths and into empowering the client for change (Kanfer and Schefft 1988). Ayelet was the one who said that I saw her and not the sickness. Focusing on her enabled her to see her own positive sources and resources.

The sixth feature, the therapist as a facilitator of change, emphasizes the important role of the therapist in pursuing effective strategies and techniques to help the client change (Rosenbaum and Ronen 1998). Ayelet feared change. I, therefore, had to push her, challenge her, and continually propose new ways for her to move toward improvement.

Finally, the seventh feature consists of empowerment and resourcefulness. All of the previous features are actually aimed at empowering clients by training them in self-control skills for self-help and independent functioning. For Ayelet, feeling independent and powerful was very important. She improved more rapidly as she learned to feel she could trust herself and that she was capable and commensurate with others.

All cognitive-constructivist interventions attempt to produce change by influencing thinking (Mahoney 1977). The techniques are designed to identify, reality-test, and correct the distorted conceptualizations and the dysfunctional beliefs (schemata) underlying these cognitions. By re-evaluating and correcting their thinking, clients learn to master problems and situations which they previously considered insuperable (Beck *et al.* 1979).

Cognitive-constructivist techniques are aimed at delineating and testing the client's specific misconceptions and maladaptive assumptions. Therefore, the client is taught to: monitor negative automatic thoughts (cognitions); recognize the connection between cognition, emotion, and behavior; examine the evidence for and against the distorted automatic thoughts; substitute more reality-oriented interpretations for these biased cognitions; and learn to identify and alter the dysfunctional beliefs that predispose the experiences (Beck *et al.* 1979).

Cognitive-Constructivist Therapy with Children and Adolescents

Cognitive-behavioral therapy with children derives from traditional behavior therapy with adults, in conjunction with cognitive components that have been adapted to the unique needs of children. It focuses on action and change and examines children's behavior, emotions, and thinking style in light of their strengths, weaknesses, and goals (Ronen 1997a, 1997b, 1998).

Cognitive therapy for children consists of a variety of techniques in which children are taught to use cognitive mediational strategies to guide their behavior and thus improve their adjustment (Durlak, Fuhrman and Lampman 1991). A wide range of cognitive-behavioral treatment strategies exists for children, many of which emphasize the manipulation of behavioral responses. Strategies may include, for example, modeling, sequential rehearsal, and skills training. The underlying target of therapy, however, consistently focuses on the cognitive distortions and deficiencies that surround the behavioral events (Powell and Oei 1991). Cognitive techniques have been proffered as a means to remediate factors that prevent youngsters from exhibiting behaviors in their repertoire, while also promoting generalization because of their reduced reliance on environmental contingencies to maintain behavior (Karoly and Kanfer 1982; Kendall and Braswell 1985).

Direct treatment of children has four main objectives (Ronen 1997a, 1997b, in press):

1. To decrease behaviors that children present too often and that disturb children as well as their environment (e.g. disobedience, negativism, impulsiveness, aggressiveness).

2. To increase behaviors that children do not present enough (e.g. social skills, assertiveness, self-esteem, self-confidence).

3. To remove anxieties that cause avoidance disorders (e.g. social fears, fear of authority, fear of separation).

4. To facilitate developmental processes (e.g. enhance children's language, self-confidence, flexibility).

With Ayelet, treatment was based mainly on the second and third objectives; that is, to increase her social skills, assertiveness, and self-esteem (second objective) and to remove her anxiety disorders (third objective).

During the last decade, I have treated children and adolescents using a combinatory method that integrates cognitive therapy and constructivist therapy. I have developed a self-control intervention package targeting children's and adolescents' disorders, which is described in the following chapter.

4
Self-Control Therapy
with Children and Adolescents

Self-control is a process occurring when, in the relative absence of immediate external constraints, a person engages in modes of behavior that had previously been less probable than had alternative available modes of behavior (Thoresen and Mahoney 1974). Self-control is called into play when new modes of behavior need to be learned, when choices need to be made, or when habitual response sequences are interrupted or prove ineffective. Self-control skills include planning, delaying gratification, use of restraint, problem solving, as well as being aware of internal sensations and emotions and allowing oneself to express emotion.

Anorexia can be conceptualized as a deficiency in the self-control skills that enable people to conduct their lives in a healthy, acceptable fashion. After the initial period of dieting, the anorexic youngster no longer has a choice about whether or not to eat. Instead, she has developed obsessive and compulsive behavior that prevents her from eating appropriately. Her actions are no longer perceived as within her control. Ayelet's behavior was no longer directed to overcome problems (such as being too fat and the need to delay temptation in order to lose weight). Instead, she was controlled by the obsession that she was not allowed to eat and should starve. The cognitive process of self-control involves several steps: the ability to notice a disruption in one's habitual (automatic, unmediated) way of thinking (Bandura 1977); the evaluation of the disruption as important for one's well-being (Rosenbaum 1993); the expectation that a specific course of action will lead to the desired outcomes; and the belief that there is a possibility for self-change (Bandura 1977).

At the stage of being an anorexic, Ayelet was no longer able to appropriately evaluate her situation. She was not looking for constructive ways to help herself change, but rather submitted herself to the feelings and thoughts of being bad, unable to cope, and wishing to die.

The targets of self-control interventions have included interpersonal thinking, means-end thinking, planning and anticipating skills, self-instruction, coping with stress, inhibiting responses, self-reinforcement, and the use of problem solving methods (Kazdin 1988). One of the earliest models of self-control was developed by Kanfer and comprised three components: self-monitoring, self-evaluation, and self-reinforcement (Kanfer and Schefft 1988).

Application of the Self-Control Model for Change

Studies on the link between children's behavior problems and self-control (Hamama, Ronen and Feigin 2000; Ronen, Wozner and Rahav 1995) led me to develop (with Wozner, 1995) an intervention model that aims to impart children and adolescents with self-control skills and to help them overcome their disorders. The model has been applied to diverse childhood disorders, and single-case designs have underscored its efficacy with problems such as sleep disorders (Ronen 1993a), encopresis (Ronen 1993b), enuresis, and stuttering (Ronen and Rosenbaum, in press). Controlled studies have also demonstrated the efficacy of the self-control model (SCM) as applied to enuresis (Ronen *et al.* 1995) and to oppositional defiant disorders (Ronen 1994).

The SCM that I have devised encompasses four modules: cognitive restructuring, problem analysis, attentional focus, and self-control practice.

Cognitive restructuring

As can be seen in the description of Ayelet's treatment in Part II, a main focus of this model concerns the attempt to teach the client that an unwanted behavior can be changed. Also, that, like many other kinds of behavior, this change depends on the client (Beck *et al.* 1979; Ellis 1962). At this point in the intervention, Ayelet learned the importance of self-efficacy (Bandura 1997). In trying to redefine her behavior, we talked about how strong she was to survive all those years and stay sane, throughout her grueling consecutive hospitalizations (rather than viewing herself as weak because she was ill). We also redefined her behavior as something she was doing to herself rather than something that had been done to her.

Problem analysis

The objective of the second skill module is to help the client understand the process that evolved into the occurrence of the identified problem. It is important to learn the links between thoughts, emotions, and behaviors as well as the link between cause and effect (Beck *et al.* 1979; Ronen 1997a, 1997b). Understanding the processes leading up to behavior has been found to be an important variable in improving clients' compliance with and adherence to treatment and also in increasing their efforts to overcome their problems (Meichenbaum and Turk 1987).

The problem analysis module is administered through rational analysis of these processes, using written materials and anatomical illustrations of the human body, and through helping the client accept responsibility for the process by learning to change the brain's commands. With Ayelet, we talked about the way her starvation was a behavior that was controlled by her automatic way of thinking (e.g. 'I must lose weight', 'I shouldn't eat'). We learned to link her behavior to her thoughts and emotions; for example, thinking about how fat she was caused her to develop stress, a low self-image, and poor self-acceptance, and self-starvation was the resulting behavior.

Attentional focus

Here clients are trained to increase awareness of their behavior in general, to raise sensitivity to the body, and particularly to identify internal cues related to the specific problem (Bandura 1969, 1997; Mahoney 1991). Although internal stimuli are difficult to identify, they have as strong an influence on behavior as do external stimuli (Bandura 1969). Awareness of internal stimuli comprises an important step towards controlling one's own behavior, in that it helps in early identification of sensations, emotions, and behaviors (Bandura 1969, 1997). Also, being aware of internal stimuli helps in changing unmediated processes into mediated ones (Kanfer and Philips 1970). Relaxation, concentration, and self-monitoring help achieve these targets.

In line with the lack of awareness and/or confusion over internal emotional and physiological states typifying girls with anorexia (Bruch 1973, 1977; Strober 1980), much of Ayelet's treatment process was devoted to this stage. Ayelet was barely aware of her own sensations and feelings. She could not identify sensations of hunger, ignored pain, and focused mainly on negative emotions. Through relaxation exercises and attentional focus exercises, she learned to become sensitive to her own bodily sensations and emotions.

Self-control practice

Within the fourth skill module, the child or adolescent is trained in self-control techniques such as self-talk, self-evaluation, self-monitoring, thinking aloud, and problem solving skills (Barrios and Hartman 1988; Brigham *et al.* 1979; Elias *et al.* 1986; Kendall and Braswell 1985; Ronen 1992, 1997a). In the first stage of general skills training, practice includes using self-instruction in the sessions and at home to overcome disappointments, and exercising self-control in day-to-day activities through homework assignments. The self-control techniques taught via this module for changing automatic behaviors to mediated ones include physical as well as emotional exercises such as resisting temptation, self-talk, self-reward, problem solving, and the use of imagery exercises (Meichenbaum 1979; Ronen 1997b). With each of her target behaviors, Ayelet was instructed to practice those skills. While overcoming fears and anxiety, she practiced exposure and self-talk. While overcoming her OCD, she practiced delaying the temptation to execute a compulsive behavior. She practiced social skills exercises to improve her social relationships, etc.

One of the main advantages of the above model is the fact that it enables maintenance and generalization of the applied learned skills. Studies pinpoint only very low drop-out and regression rates for the SCM (Ronen et al. 1995). Also, the model's foci on empowerment and the development of independent functioning are conducive to transference of learned competencies. A case in point was the single-case study on a child treated for his enuresis with SCM, who then continued on to effectively apply the learned skills and stop biting his nails without therapeutic intervention (Ronen and Rosenbaum, in press). Ayelet, as well, mastered assorted self-control skills through the treatment process and was able to use them in coping with unfamiliar later situations, without the need to return to treatment. There was no regression in her condition, nor did she need additional interventions for other problems she faced in her work, while raising her children, and in her relationship with her husband.

PART V

Guidelines for Therapists

Cognitive Creative Intervention with Anorexic Clients

Embarking on the treatment of an anorexic client necessitates a careful consideration of:

1. the disorder's manifestations in the referred client

2. the client's particular developmental features

3. the client's personal and environmental characteristics

4. aspects of the therapist's orientation and background.

Relating to the disorder itself, the features to be considered include the client's stage of illness, the severity of the illness, and its specific cognitive, emotional, and behavioral manifestations in this individual client. Relating to developmental considerations, the therapist should reflect on the client's age, the characteristics of anorexia in this specific age group, and the kind of behavior that characterizes youngsters of this age group. For example, children's characteristics and needs differ from those of adolescents or adults. Relating to the client's personal and environmental variables, the therapist must observe the client's particular attributes, special or unique qualities, strengths, and available internal resources, as well as their external sources of familial, social, and community support. Relating to therapist variables, therapists should be well aware of their preferred basic ground theory and of the repertoire of techniques they can offer. All of the above areas in need of mindful deliberation would, in themselves, suffice for an entire separate volume. In the next pages, I will try to elaborate on at least some of the major, unique components therapists should consider in their encounter with an anorexic client.

I

Making Decisions about the Need for Therapy

Treating anorexic adolescents may be seen as a particularly complex process, due to the complications typifying anorexia, the inherent complexity of adolescence, and the challenging intricacy of treating children and adolescents in general. These three areas of complexity, outlined below, call for a careful and accurate process of assessment, which contributes to the first step in determining a need for therapy.

With regard to the first aspect of complexity, as I discussed in Part IV (Chapter 1), the most distressing aspect of treating anorexia may be the life-menacing nature of the disorder, implying an even greater responsibility than may usually be placed on the therapist's shoulders. Additional complications of the disorder that I described previously include the anorexic client's tendency to resist treatment, to deny the danger, and to resist change.

The second complex feature relates to the unique nature of the adolescent stage. Adolescents may be seen as constantly changing, typified by predictably dynamic changes and unstable emotional, cognitive, and behavioral processes. Teenagers generally opt not to have therapy because of its stigma and their fear of embarrassment if friends were to find out. They also tend to fear therapy in general, demonstrating age-typical anxiety about the therapist's 'magical' or mind-reading powers. Moreover, they tend to be preoccupied with separation and individuation from parent figures, and with the search for independence and the development of their own identity. These age-related tasks may interfere with adolescents' ability to trust the therapist as a significant adult. Anorexic teenagers, in particular, view the therapist as someone who is against them, in light of the therapist's wish to stop their self-starvation. Therapy, therefore, is very complicated and complex (Ronen 1997b).

With respect to the third area of complexity in treating children and adolescents in general, I have dealt with this issue at length in my book *Cognitive Developmental Therapy with Children* (Ronen 1997b). I reviewed, there, the main steps via which therapists should proceed while assessing children and making decisions about the need for therapy. That review underscored a number of factors relating to the nature of the client, the nature of the problem, family and environmental components, and prognostic criteria. Among these factors, I will present several guidelines here, adapted specifically to assessment of the anorexic client:

Problem Variables

1. *Compare the client's presented behavior with accepted diagnostic criteria.* The most frequently used criteria for anorexia consist of the DSM-IV (American Psychiatric Association 1994). These criteria help define the disorder, utilizing indices based on the duration of the problem, severity of impairment, and number of dysfunctional behaviors. The standardized diagnostic manuals also provide important information on features associated with anorexia nervosa, and predisposing factors. Looking at the assessment process with Ayelet, although she had received many additional diagnoses, she fits all of the criteria for anorexia according to the DSM-IV.

2. *Assess the stability of the problem.* Almost all girls diet at one time or another. Almost all adolescents have problems relating to their self-acceptance and self-esteem. It is even popular to be on a diet as a teenager, and it may seem strange for youngsters not to question or doubt the way they behave. It is important to assess the seriousness and stability of the client's dieting regimen and self-esteem and sexual identity problems. Questions concerning the perseverance of problem behaviors

should be addressed by collecting historical data from the family and, if necessary, the school. The stability of behavior should serve as a guideline for determining whether or not a referred child needs therapy. Ayelet had been dieting for many years, since the age of 14. Her behavior clearly did not represent a merely temporary attempt to diet, but rather had steadily endured for a long period of her life. Also, her anxiety and feelings of poor self-worth disturbed her and dominated her life.

Client Variables

1. *Compare the client's presented behavior with environmental norms.* In evaluating the client's anorexic behavior, it is important to assess whether the client's peers behave similarly. Does the behavior characterize most others in the client's peer group, or does it deviate from the client's immediate environment? Ayelet's behavior significantly deviated from that of her environment, as shown in her teachers' and peers' responses and her own feelings of aloneness, loneliness, and social isolation.

2. *Compare the client's presented behavior with age norms.* In light of the constant changes typifying adolescence, clients referred for anorexia should also be evaluated to determine whether their behavior is age-appropriate, resembling normative behavior among children their age. Although dieting characterizes young female adolescents, Ayelet's regimen was significantly more rigid and limiting, and her behavior was not characteristic for her age group.

3. *Evaluate the client's motivation.* As difficult as anorexia is, treatment can be very successful once the client suffering from the disorder develops the motivation to change. It is much more difficult to treat clients who do not wish to enter therapy and who do not comply with it. This feature is critical while considering the kind of setting in which to treat clients. In applying treatments by law or force in a hospital setting (as

Ayelet had been hospitalized by a court injunction), anorexic clients could be forced to eat or may be restrained in a closed unit. However, in a private clinic, it is almost impossible to treat self-destructive clients who resist therapy and who do not comply with basic rules that help them stay alive.

4. *Identify the client's strengths, positive qualities and resources.* An important issue relating to the success of therapy concerns the client's positive capacities. Various features should be assessed, including how the client coped with past difficulties, what type of persuasive tactics might be effective for this particular client, which figures are significant for the client, and what hobbies and activities are favored by the client. Such features can provide clues as to how to help the client change and as to who can play an important part in this change process. Ayelet was not motivated for therapy focusing explicitly on gaining weight. However, her poor self-esteem and feeling of being deviant in her world motivated her to 'improve and become a better person'. Those goals corresponded with a more generally focused, cognitive-constructivist therapeutic mode.

Familial and Environmental Variables

Identify the client's support systems. The support system can play a crucial role in treating anorexic clients, particularly when motivation is lacking. It is virtually impossible to conduct effective therapy without the intensive help and support of the parents. Ayelet's parents loved her a great deal. They did not know how to help her, but their readiness and willingness to try suggested that I would be able to involve them as active partners in therapy. Also, Ayelet's grandmother was a very important figure in her life, challenging her to recover.

Prognostic Criteria

1. *Assess future risk to the client.* An important consideration when determining the need for therapy during childhood consists of

evaluating the extent of risk to which the child will be exposed in the future if the disorder is left untreated. In the case of anorexia, it should be determined whether the identified problem stems from the parents' exaggerated concern or over-anxiousness, or whether it resembles the beginnings of a true anorexic process. The diet should be evaluated as to whether it is a healthy, appropriate one or a dangerous one. Ayelet was still at physical risk when I met her. It was important to stop the dieting process as soon as possible in order to enable her to live a healthy life.

2. *Assess anticipated responsiveness to treatment.* Decisions as to whether or not to treat often depend on prognostic implications (Achenbach 1985). Two projections should be developed: (a) regarding whether the behaviors are likely to remain the same, improve, or deteriorate in the absence of treatment; and (b) regarding whether that outcome will differ as a function of differing treatments. With anorexic clients, it is sometimes impossible to apply therapy without hospitalization due to the way they risk their lives and may be in danger of dying. Although Ayelet's past history did not show improvement, I believed she could cooperate and improve in therapy. I did not believe she really wanted to die, and I thought that if I found the right way to involve her and challenge her to work toward change, a possibility would open up for her to respond differently to therapy than previously.

The four aforementioned criteria – problem variables, client variables, familial and environmental variables, and prognostic criteria – should serve as a basis for the therapist's first decision as to whether or not the client requires treatment. In Ayelet's case, all of these criteria indicated the need for therapy and the potential for successful treatment. The second therapeutic decision, described in the following chapter, consists of determining the optimal setting(s) for treating the client.

2

Making Decisions about the
Appropriate Setting(s) for Change

Assessments of the client's disorder, strengths, and environmental resources, as described in the previous chapter, answer the question: Who should be treated? They also provide a foundation for dealing with the second step in therapeutic decision making, which addresses the question: How should that client be treated? Many possibilities are available, including family therapy, parent counseling, individual treatment, group therapy, etc.

Because I view anorexia as a multidimensional problem, I refute the advisability of individual treatment as the sole setting. Individual treatment of an anorexic client is very important, mainly for helping the client change self-evaluation, self-acceptance, and body image. However, anorexia is very strongly rooted in family relationships. The way parents relate to their child's eating habits and the way they deal with their child's emotional processes have a heavy influence on the development and maintenance of the disorder. Therefore, there is a need to combine individual therapy with parent counseling and family therapy. Moreover, beyond the involvement of parents in the treatment process, significant others such as friends, relatives, and siblings may offer an effective support system for the client. Establishing a strong support system, increasing social skills, and fostering social involvement are also important for anorexic clients. Such relationships with family members and significant others should have been evaluated (see above) in the first step of decision making.

As mentioned earlier, Ayelet's treatment was designed to begin with a combination of parental supervision and family therapy, in order to provide Ayelet with strong support from her family to help her invest effort in the change process. Only subsequently was individual treatment initiated. Much later in therapy, when her boyfriend (whom she later married) became her most important resource and support system, we involved him in therapy as well.

3

Treatment Considerations and Adaptations

In attempting to increase the likelihood of success in the complex, difficult treatment of anorexic clients, the therapist should take into consideration several important issues during intervention planning. Issues to be considered include: ways to increase and maintain client motivation; ways to involve the environment in the treatment; ways to adapt multiple treatment techniques to the individual client's needs, style, and interests; and the ability to be flexible and to apply creative thinking to the intervention.

Increasing Client Motivation for Change

Kanfer and Schefft (1988) claimed that everyone is motivated. It is the therapist's challenge to discover what the client is motivated for, and to try to design therapy to increase motivation. As mentioned earlier, anorexic clients are generally not motivated for change, and they often arrive at therapy because they were coerced by someone rather than from their own free will. It is the therapist's responsibility to work toward increasing motivation in all stages of therapy (Ronen 1997b). Motivation can take the form of offering clients, at last, a place that accepts them as they are; additionally, motivation can be elevated by an atmosphere of collaboration between client and therapist. In the first stages of treatment, it is sometimes necessary to make anorexic adolescents do things they do not wish to do. For example, they might be asked to talk with their parents despite a disinterest in such conversation; to start meeting peers again although they would rather not; or to make an effort to start eating even though they wish to lose weight. However, honesty, respect, involvement in the process of therapy, and explanations of treatment techniques and methods might contribute to compliance and collaboration.

As I described above, Ayelet was unmotivated to gain weight, but she was suffering greatly from her problems and was motivated to become a better person and to change what she thought of as her 'bad character and bad drives'. Mobilizing her own goals, I engaged her in investing efforts toward achieving her aims for the treatment. Furthermore, from the beginning, I offered clear, open explanations of my interventions and actively involved Ayelet in her own assessment and treatment process. From her account of that period, it seems that Ayelet's active participation elicited in her a sense of self-worth and served to enhance her enthusiasm and optimism about the treatment.

Ways to Involve the Environment in the Treatment

As mentioned earlier, anorexia is not a single, sole problem. It is a holistic disorder that includes whole areas of life. It relates to personal components (self-acceptance, self-image, thinking styles); family relationships and family attitudes toward life in general and toward the client in particular; social relationships and peer acceptance. Often, the environment (friends or teachers) are the first to identify the disorder. With Ayelet, her teachers and peers noticed the change in her weight long before her parents could acknowledge it. The involvement of the environment in the treatment, when possible, can facilitate positive change. This refers, of course, to the important venues of parent counseling and family therapy, but also to the involvement of the school and friends. For example, educational counselors and school nurses may implement educational interventions with the client's whole class on eating habits, the dangers of dieting, or self-acceptance issues. Group therapy can help in applying social skills. Also, it is important to encourage the youngster to become involved in social activities by challenging the client to call friends, to start participating in a youth group, to attend class parties, and the like. Ayelet had desisted from all peer activity, and, unfortunately, her interpersonal relations revolved mostly around other sick youngsters she met in the various hospitals.

Adapting Techniques to the Client's Communication Level and Style

The treatment of adolescents necessitates a collaboration with their style, language, and way of thinking in order to mobilize them as active partners in the change process. These communicational requirements imply that therapists treating children and adolescents must participate actively in the client's natural environment, become familiar with the important figures in the client's life, and be flexible in the use of different methods for helping the client. Therapists must be keenly sensitive to the client's language in order to use it for communication in therapy. It is important to maintain awareness of the client's personal style of thinking and talking, rather than to impose techniques that are unlikely to be accepted by this specific client. For example, Ayelet's manner of communicating, verbally and through her drawings and writings, was laden with metaphors and images. I did not impose this treatment technique, but rather listened carefully, identified her metaphoric style, and tried to utilize metaphors as a mode for facilitating change.

Regardless of the therapist's personal inclinations or theoretical orientations, incorporating the client's personal terminology serves as an important base of reference in therapeutic communication with the client. For example, I could not tell Ayelet: 'Hey, I am a cognitive therapist. I don't deal with big black holes or dark nothings. Those belong to psychodynamic intervention.' Rather, I tried to collaborate with her language, enter those big black holes of emptiness, and fill them. Using her kind of language, her metaphors, and her images helped me collaborate with her and helped Ayelet trust me, despite her suspiciousness due to her disillusionment with many previous treatments and therapists.

Matching Therapists' Theories and Techniques to Clients' Needs and Interests

Although verbal therapy is the treatment of choice with adolescents, drawing, playing, or exercises may be employed to increase their enthusiastic involvement. Yet care should be taken to ensure that nonverbal, indirect methods are not perceived as insulting to the young person who wishes to be treated as an adult. Although determined in part by limitations in the therapist's technical repertoire, the therapist's selection of techniques should consider a variety of factors, including the youngster's interests, preferences, and developmental stage (Brandell 1992; Ronen 1992). This includes tuning into the client's specific interests and day-to-day experiences in order to more fully understand the context in which familiar content areas are described. Subjects familiar to the client can then be used as effective analogies for relating to and explaining cognitive, emotional, and behavioral processes. Ayelet's enjoyment of drawing and writing enabled me to ask her, for instance, to draw her emotions, to write a letter to her parents, or to try and rewrite her own life story by giving it another end. Such assignments might raise rejection in an adolescent who hates to draw or who is uncomfortable with written self-expression.

As a cognitive-behavioral therapist, I view therapy as a scientific process of problem solving. I believe in empirical measurement of outcomes. I view behavioral and cognitive therapies not as techniques but as a way of life, as a theoretical approach, and as a way of looking at one's behavior and trying to change it (Ronen 1997b). With adolescents in general, and anorexic clients in particular, therapists should always ask themselves: What would I like to achieve? Which technique or method can best help my client at this stage? What technique or method could match this client's thinking style, hobbies, and lifestyle?

For instance, the utilization of cognitive techniques to modify Ayelet's misconceptions would have only increased her resistance. She felt fat and ugly and would not accept attempts to change her.

Rather than trying to work on change, then, a more effective technique would be to target self-acceptance using, for example, a constructivist technique of collaborating with her automatic misconceptions. I told Ayelet: 'Well, it isn't easy to be fat and ugly. But let's check if ugly, fat people can find a place for themselves in the world, and what it means to live like that.'

Only by collaborating with Ayelet's meaning-making process of the disorder and the change process, could I help her find new meaning in her life, and a wish to improve.

4

Applying Constructivist Creative Intervention

A distinction may be made between the therapist as a technician and the therapist as an artist (Mahoney 1991). A therapist should not only master theories and techniques, but should also be an expert on human change processes and human characteristics. Most of all, therapists should be able to determine which intervention is the treatment of choice for each client in each situation. The ability to be flexible (Kanfer and Schefft 1988) and the capacity for creativity are qualities that help therapists tap their artistic potential. A creative psychotherapist is one who can adapt the treatment process to the client's unique and individual needs – using the modes, strategies, and techniques that best suit the client's way of thinking, or designing a new intervention from which the client can learn and benefit the most.

Much literature has been written on how to learn to be creative, what makes people creative, and how to facilitate creativity. Mahoney (1991) described the creative psychotherapist as one who helps clients explore and experience themselves and the world in different ways. These new ways challenge ordinary, familiar patterns and consolidate embodiment, emotion, feeling, sensing, and thinking into one entity. Clarkson (1995) proposed that a creative therapist is one who is called upon to compare and contrast the differing ways that a client can make the world cohere, rather than one who avoids this demand. The task is to help clients conceive order out of personal chaos; that is, to help them transform personal confusion and pain into a more meaningful, fulfilling life plan.

Creative intervention involves an ability to attack a problem from a new direction, which implies flexibility of thought. Brainstorming techniques for facilitating creativity, for example, rule out criticism, welcome the freewheeling, seek quantity, and improve and complement suggestions (Weisberg 1992). Weisberg presented a table of methods for increasing creativity such as list making, questioning assumptions, attribute listing, analogies, incubation, and problem solving. Other guides for creativity include skills such as breaking out of old patterns or ways of thinking, keeping options open, suspending judgement, thinking broadly, breaking out of scripts, taking fresh perspectives, and using tricks.

Kopp (1995) proposed two approaches to working with metaphors. Client-generated metaphors are exercised when the therapist identifies the client's metaphorical language and tries to use it in therapy. Therapist-generated metaphors are exercised when the client does not naturally use metaphors, but the therapist believes metaphors can be of help and proposes them to the client. Metaphoric methods may thus be quite acceptable and enlightening, even for clients who do not intuitively generate such symbolic language.

Realizing that Ayelet deeply enjoyed a creative way of talking, thinking, and producing art, I tried to keep on par with her level and diversity of creativity. My active attunement to her drawings, writings, metaphors, and images enabled me to select innovative and varied interventions that succeeded in raising her curiosity, mobilizing her motivation for change, and maintaining that motivation over the lengthy, often arduous period of treatment.

5

Focusing on the
Therapeutic Relationship

Ayelet used to say that I was the first person who treated her as a human being rather than treating her problem. What she really meant was that we succeeded in establishing a trusting, honest, equal relationship. I believe that our therapeutic relationship was the most effective tool in her treatment.

The therapeutic relationship is important in every change process. However, it has crucial significance in individual therapy during adolescence (Brandell 1992). Children as well as adolescents will not continue treatment if they are bored or cannot easily express themselves, or if the therapist does not succeed in stimulating their curiosity, motivation, and participation (Kazdin 1988; Ronen 1992). The therapist must create a climate of trust and establish a meaningful emotional relationship with the client (Rose and Edelson 1988). These tenets may hold doubly true for the resistant, suspicious, and reluctant anorexic teenager brought to therapy by concerned parents.

The therapeutic relationship can be seen as a framework that encompasses the entire treatment process. This holds true in general, and even more so in working with anorexic clients. For anorexics, a trusting, collaborative relationship is imperative to the establishment of the primary contract during assessment and of the treatment contract later on. A good therapeutic relationship creates trust, openness, and a willingness to cooperate in the client. It is a prerequisite even in the earliest stages of assessment. A good relationship helps achieve an efficient assessment process, the reliable collection of data from all parties involved, an accurate diagnosis, and appropriate decision making regarding whether the client needs therapy. Without a good therapeutic relationship, the therapist will find it very difficult to foster adolescents' open expression, acknowledgement, and sharing of their problems and concerns.

The growing recognition of the importance of emotion has led to an increased accentuation of internal processes and a sharper focus on emotions, and, as a result, on treatment processes and therapeutic relationships (Mahoney 1991, 1995). Mahoney emphasized the importance of the therapeutic relationship both with respect to the therapist and to the client. He suggested that psychotherapy is a difficult and complex challenge for both therapist and client, proposing that therapists change during the treatment process at least as much as clients do. The treatment process, according to him, is an emotional experience for both parties. Rosenbaum and Ronen (1998) and Ronen and Rosenbaum (1998) emphasized that the therapeutic relationship is influenced by expectations, ways of thinking, and schemata that both the therapist and client bring to the therapeutic interaction.

The first time I felt that there was really a chance that I could help Ayelet occurred when she did not show up for a session. She had stayed home because she was afraid to harm me. That gave me a first clue that some emotional relationship had begun to develop between the two of us. As we continued on to create a good, trusting, caring relationship, I could earn her confidence and thus assure her that she would be safe while following me along the difficult path toward change.

6

Incorporating Emotional Processes into Cognitive-Behavioral Therapy

For many years, behavioral as well as cognitive theories focused on changing thoughts and behaviors, and highlighted the need to impart clients with coping skills. This resulted in an emphasis on externalizing rather than internalizing disorders. For example, hyperactive and impulsive children were taught techniques for delaying gratification and overcoming temptation (Kendall and Braswell 1985), clients were instructed in methods to overcome fears and phobias (Marks 1987), etc. The treatment of anorexia has traditionally focused on eating habits and on techniques to facilitate weight gain (Siegel and Smith 1991). Emotional problems underlying the disorder (such as self-acceptance or body image) were not a central focus of therapy.

Constructivist therapy contributed significantly to the study of emotional processes. This approach advocated a shift in focus from the problem to the person, emphasizing the individual's personal, subjective construction of events. As a result, there has been a dramatic increase in the study of the role of emotion in human functioning (Safran and Segal 1990) and a shift of interest from externalizing to internalizing disorders. Studies over the last decade relating to emotional processes have underscored the role of emotions for human development in general (Greenberg and Safran 1987; Hayes *et al.* 1994; Mahoney 1991; Neimeyer and Mahoney 1995; Safran and Segal 1990). Emotions are particularly important in understanding development during childhood and adolescence

(Bailey 1998; Barkley 1997; Finch *et al.* 1993; Herbert 1998; Kazdin 1987; Shirk and Russell 1996).

Emotion in the process of development has been viewed both as a product of, and as a process in, social interaction and everyday experiences (Parker 1994). Emotional development is reflected by a gradual increase in children's ability to show signs of emotion. As this develops, the child is capable of talking about emotions and showing an enhanced understanding of emotional terms. It then becomes easier for the child to understand situations that elicit emotion, to induce emotions in themselves and others, to understand emotional cues, and to integrate successive or simultaneous emotions (Terwogt and Olthof 1989).

In fact, emotion regulation is one of the first major developmental challenges for the human infant. Children learn to struggle to organize their multiple biological systems, via the way they differently experience and express issues relating to emotion. The most important facilitation children receive in their emotional development is from a sensitive and responsive caregiver who first helps infants settle into and create basic patterns of behavior and emotion. Emotions are elicited through the development of attachment.

Children with internalizing disorders have been pinpointed by the recent decade's body of research as a group at risk for future impairment (Finch *et al.* 1993; Herbert 1998; Kazdin 1987; Shirk and Russell 1996).

Researchers proposed that such children may gain from treatment that is directed to emotional components. Illustrations of such components include the need to identify emotions, the ability to express emotions, the need to accept others' emotions, and the need to be empathic with others as well as with oneself.

In the last few years, cognitive therapists have become significantly more aware of and able to recognize the priority of feeling in shaping our knowing and doing (Mahoney 1999). More intense efforts are being concentrated on ways to better understand our emotional processes and to address such processes in cognitive therapy by urging clients to deal with, handle, and change emotions. Emotional change and internalizing disorders have become a central core of cognitive and constructivist therapy.

An understanding of the anorexic client's emotional processes enables the therapist to focus treatment on emotional deficits, deprivation, or distortion rather than to focus mainly on behavior change. As she entered therapy, Ayelet was clearly a very emotional person. She was keenly tuned in to others' feelings and distorted her own emotional processes and beliefs. An important part of treating Ayelet was the focus on urging her to relate to, discuss, and identify her internal cues. She worked on listening and developing the ability to identify various sensations such as hunger or thirst, and on learning to identify the differentiation between feeling too full (i.e. not needing to eat) and being stressed and angry (and therefore not wanting to eat). Learning to accept her emotions, as well as witnessing my ability to let her share my emotions, she collaborated with me toward an effective process of change.

7

Challenging Clients to Open Up to New Experiences

Infants grow and develop within a constant interplay between two forces: opening up to and closing up to experiences. In the first step of development, babies open up to themselves as well as to the environment that surrounds them. They explore and experience new behaviors, sensations, or emotions. Very young children look around curiously, ready to meet each new and unknown stimulus. They become acquainted with experiences through their senses: they look at, taste, smell, touch, and listen to stimuli (Ronen 1992). At the same time, they naturally learn to stop or avoid strongly unpleasant stimuli. For example, they close their eyes when a light is too bright, and they cry when startled by a loud noise.

The other force that transpires during growth consists of the ability to close oneself off from experiences: to evaluate, restrain, and inhibit responses (Rosenbaum 1999). As they get older, children are taught by adults to limit their automatic, unmediated behavior and to minimize their spontaneous reactions to experiences (Ronen 1992), prevent impulsive behavior, restrain from certain actions, delay gratification, and think before they act (Kendall and Braswell 1985). Barkley (1997) claimed that humans have evolved the capability to delay and inhibit initial prepotent responses. This ability serves as an important developmental task. Inhibition of response enables infants to create a mental representation of the event in mind. Mental representation is followed by the 'working memory', which, in turn, facilitates the use of cognitive skills for information processing. Human development, therefore, involves an interplay between opening up to experiences followed by closing off from and evaluating experiences.

Human beings develop by being active and reactive toward themselves as well as toward the world they live in. Activity is a process of nonstop exploring, experiencing, and giving meaning to occurrences. Experiencing and exploration help people open up to what life brings to them, dare, take chances, be willing to change, and keep open to the world and to themselves. By experiencing and exploring, individuals learn, sense, and experience themselves in the world, become aware, and look for meaning. The process of exploration from within the individual leads to a developmentally progressive understanding of the world (Mahoney 1991). Mahoney emphasized the importance of exploration as a normal urge of human beings as well as a necessity for helping one change, recover, and develop.

Rosenbaum (1993, 1999) described healthy human behavior as the capacity to be flexible in shifting between opening and closing responses. Opening responses involve the ability of the individual to be attuned to experiences (external as well as internal) without judging them. Closing responses encompass the process of attributing meaning to experiences, constructing them, relating them to past experiences, and directing the kind and amount of experience one explores. The shift between opening and closing responses actually constitutes a flexible behavior that combines facing experiences openly with the process of thinking. By sustaining a healthy flexibility, individuals keep attuned to themselves and the world as well as maintain self-control.

Many disturbances can be attributed to difficulties in shifting between opening and closing responses. Human beings can be too open, frequently searching for novel emotional experiences while lacking necessary mediated, cognitive responses such as thinking and evaluating. At the other end of the spectrum, people can be overly preoccupied with the need to observe, evaluate, and plan behavior while avoiding internal openness to emotional experiences and external exploration of new worlds. Either of these extremes prevents the flexibility to gradually shift and change responses.

One of Ayelet's difficulties consisted of her fear of opening up to experiences. She avoided opening up to the world and closed herself in her own small world. She refused to do anything unfamiliar, or things that evoked the slightest feeling of incompetence or a lack of full control. Ayelet commonly used closing off responses: analyzing, evaluating, looking ahead, and planning her future steps. She was unwilling to use opening up responses in order to just try to explore and experience life. Therapy with Ayelet gradually challenged her to enlarge her experience, learn to explore the world, and try to open up to what life brought her.

8

Designing the Process of Intervention

As described in detail in Part II of this book, Gambrill and colleagues (1971) proposed procedural guidelines in order to help therapists facilitate effective intervention. In their 12-step procedure, each step comprises three components: its objective, rationale, and means of operation. These steps help the therapist organize the intervention process. Whereas the content of intervening with Ayelet varied from one session to the next, the process of intervention followed this 12-step procedure, in order to structure our therapeutic work.

1. *Inventory of problem areas.* The objective of this step is to gather information related to the client's whole spectrum of problems, and its rationale is to devise a problem area profile. The means of operation consist of accumulating full descriptions of presenting problems, and then organizing them into different problem areas (i.e. placing several related problems together under one heading) (Ronen 1997b). Following this step enabled me to make sense of Ayelet's long list of problems. We recorded all her problems, decided which ones corresponded to similar areas, and devised a list of problematic areas.

2. *Problem selection and contract.* In this step, client–therapist agreement on problem areas is reached, and the first specific area for treatment is selected. In line with the above objectives, the rationale for this step is to stimulate the client's cooperation and involvement. The means of intervention consist of conversing about the problem list and negotiating

the selection. After the first intake session, I discussed with Ayelet and her parents the long list of problem areas and proposed to start therapy with family treatment in order to improve how Ayelet felt at home. As Ayelet and her parents agreed, we established a contract relating to the sequence and content of therapy.

3. *Commitment to cooperate.* The third step aims to obtain client agreement to cooperate with the process, facilitating compliance. Means of operation include providing explanations, reading the agreement, and asking for agreement. Ayelet's treatment required two kinds of commitment: parental agreement to cooperate with the family therapy and to enable Ayelet to work together with me individually; and Ayelet's own agreement to comply with the multisetting therapeutic process. As previously mentioned, anorexic clients are often not interested in therapy. It is impossible to treat them without obtaining their commitment to cooperate. If not regarding the issue of weight increase, at least a commitment to attending sessions, trying to improve family relationships, or learning to feel better with themselves.

4. *Specification of target behaviors.* In this step, specific details are collected concerning the selected problem, with a focus on what maintains and reinforces the problem (Ronen 1997b). The multitreatment design for Ayelet implied that each time we began working in another setting or on another issue (family therapy, parent counseling, treating anxiety, fears, and OCD, etc.), we decided on the specific goals to attain. For example, while working with the family, we specified the following goals: facilitating the family members' direct communication with one another and their ability to talk about emotions; attempting to decrease the anger and distrust; and fostering the development of trusting relationships.

5. *Baseline of target behavior.* In the fifth step, the problem's pre-intervention frequency and duration are determined, in

order to provide a concrete basis for evaluating change through records and estimation. Kazdin (1982) emphasized the importance of baseline information for validating data collection, and for ascertaining in depth all the antecedents, maintenance, and outcomes relating to behavior. Each time we selected a new goal for therapy, Ayelet (and often her parents) recorded features of the specific behavior, to provide data on its frequency, intensity, and current manifestation. These recordings contributed to the specification of appropriate techniques targeting change, as well as to the evaluation process.

6. *Identification of problem-controlling conditions.* The aim of the sixth step is to learn the conditions preceding and following the problem's occurrence. Records are maintained of incidents transpiring before, during, and after the problem's occurrence, thus demonstrating the importance of discriminatory stimuli affecting the problem. For example, to learn what maintained Ayelet's OCD, she recorded surrounding incidents. It emerged that, each time she counted, she felt a decrease in anxiety, which reinforced her to perform more counting in the future. Another example can be drawn from her thoughts. Each time Ayelet would refer to the voices she heard, her therapists related to them as a bizarre behavior, a symptom of her illness, and they tried to teach her ways to change her thoughts. Ayelet learned that something was wrong with her. The more time she spent in therapy, the more she developed the idea that she was bad, had to be changed, and maybe was crazy. We learned to link her thoughts to her emotions, and we came to see her suicide attempts and continuous weight loss as resulting from her fears of the bad drives and urges she felt she had.

7. *Assessment of environmental resources.* The seventh step aims to identify possible resources in the client's environment. Without enlisting the environment's help, change is difficult to induce. This step is conducted by asking the client or by interviewing

significant others or agents in the environment. Ayelet had many resources, both external and internal. External resources included her parents, grandmother, and boyfriend. She also evidenced many internal resources: her creativity, sensitivity, wisdom, and much more.

8. *Specification of behavioral objectives.* The eighth step aims to specify the behavioral objectives of the modification plan. It elicits the client's terminal behavioral repertoire. In the beginning of Ayelet's intervention, it was impossible to specify the behavioral objectives because she was uninterested in change. After a time, she became able to talk about objectives like: to stop losing weight, feel better, stop feeling cold, and improve her relationships with her parents. Later on, we could add many more objectives.

9. *Formulation of a modification plan.* The ninth step focuses on selecting an appropriate technique – the most efficient program for change. The means to achieve this selection comprises reviewing the information in the aforementioned steps and examining available interventions. For Ayelet's multitreatment design, I was unable to select only one main method or technique for change. Instead, I shared with Ayelet my beliefs about the way people change, that is, my cognitive-constructivist framework. Then, each time I intended to use a specific technique, I explained its purpose and method, and asked for her agreement.

10. *Implementation of modification plan.* The tenth step focuses on modifying the behavior. It concentrates effort on change and on conducting a specific intervention technique. Ayelet's intervention process was lengthy, gradual, and variable throughout its application. However, we always planned our objectives and our path toward achieving them.

11. *Monitoring outcomes.* The eleventh step aims at obtaining information concerning the effectiveness of intervention. It provides feedback on effectiveness and also increases the client

motivation. In each of Ayelet's sessions, we would assess outcomes. For example, we constantly assessed how anxious she was during the last week in comparison with prior weeks; how obsessed she was in relation to how obsessed she had been previously; whether or not she improved her eating habits that week; and so on. This became an important method for increasing Ayelet's motivation to change and for mobilizing her cooperation.

12. *Maintenance of change.* The twelfth step aims to achieve maintenance and stabilization. It helps prevent relapses and uses the environment for maintenance or a specific plan. For example, through therapy, the parents were instructed not to interfere with Ayelet's eating habits and not to talk or force her to eat. However, near the end of therapy I was interested in evaluating how Ayelet would react if her parents failed to follow these instructions. (To explore her feelings and increase her readiness to cope, we talked about how she thought she would react if they talked about her eating, looked at her plate, or tried to force her to eat.) Maintenance was achieved by continuing follow-up sessions with Ayelet almost a year after we terminated therapy. We continued meeting once every six to eight weeks to deal with new events, follow up on her behavior, and ensure that there was no regression.

9

Applying the Self-Control Model for Change

As described in the literature review in Part IV, treatment of Ayelet followed my self-control model (SCM) for change. This model aimed to provide Ayelet with self-control skills that would improve her functioning. In this section, I will specify how I applied each of the SCM's several modules to Ayelet: cognitive restructuring, problem analysis, attentional focus, and self-control practice.

Cognitive restructuring

In order to help teach Ayelet that her unwanted behavior could be changed, and that this change depended on her (Beck *et al.* 1979; Ellis 1962), I had to redefine Ayelet's behavior. Rather than up-holding her view of herself as someone very weak due to her fears, anxieties, and OCD, I emphasized that she was a very strong person who had survived all those hospitalizations and still remained sane, strong, and creative. Rather than supporting her self-perception as a bad person who had evil drives and had tried to kill herself, I helped her redefine her problems. I encouraged her to talk about her good nature, her constant desire to improve, and her fear that she was not good enough. We redefined her behavior as paying a price for caring so much and wishing to be such a good human being. We reframed her craziness, hallucinations, and delusions in terms of self-talk that consistently urged her to achieve change. We used Socratic questions and paradoxical examples to foster her understanding that her problems were a function of motivation and will power, rather than of bad luck or illness.

Problem analysis

Ayelet's treatment attempted to teach her to observe the connections between her brain, body, and final problematic behaviors. For example, we talked about the way the thought of eating was interpreted by her as something bad, as something she should avoid because it caused her to gain weight. This interpretation elicited a whole list of negative emotions (stress, frustration) and negative sensations (stomach aches, a feeling of fullness in her throat). The outcome was her behavior: the wish to vomit, stop eating, and continue using medications to empty herself. We focused on learning to notice the links between thoughts, emotions, and behaviors and to learn the link between cause and effect (Beck *et al.* 1979; Ronen 1997a, 1997b). I believed that it would be easier for her to change her behavior after understanding how the problem behaviors emerged and how they were affected by different thoughts and feelings. For example, the ability to change the thought from 'I should not eat, it is bad for me' to 'Maybe I could eat a little bit and it won't hurt me' might change the emotion from stress and anger to willingness and cooperation. The expected outcome of the behavior might therefore be changed from vomiting to eating a little. We practiced the identification of her anxious automatic thoughts. We used self-talk and self-recording to change her wish for compulsive behavior, and we practiced changing unmediated thoughts into mediated ones.

Attentional focus

Ayelet practiced listening to her body, e.g. learning to identify the cues of hunger and her internal sensations of fear or anxiety, learned to differentiate the cues of hunger from the cues relating to other kinds of stomach aches. She learned to differentiate between stress, anxiety, fears and the more positive experience of excitement.

Self-control practice

Throughout the whole intervention process, Ayelet was instructed to practice new skills such as self-talk and exposure exercises such as going outside for increasing lengths of time and distances. Through practice, she learned that, as confidence grows, the chances of success also increase (Bandura 1997).

IO

Fostering Maintenance and Generalization

Ayelet is not the only client who has experienced a long list of therapists and medications. As with other disorders, the drop-out and regression rates for anorexic clients often prevent a successful process of therapy. Treatment of anorexia, therefore, should be long-term, should focus on overlearning and maintenance, and must include a follow-up stage in order to avoid regression.

Several methods have been devised to help maintain outcomes and avoid regression. One consists of using multiple trials in different settings and tasks. In other words, the client is followed in settings other than the therapeutic one, with different people and regarding different behaviors (such as home, friends, work). Another method anticipates potential as well as real failures and coordinates them into the intervention program; and a performance-based rather than time-based termination of training may also be effective. Robin (1985) suggested the use of solutions, additional discussions, or debates to be held at home, and also recommended tasks incorporating newly acquired skills or attitudes into daily living. Rose and Edelson (1988) differentiated between strategies for the generalization of actions that occur within the intervention setting (e.g. increasing responsibilities, varying examples, preparing for setbacks, conceptualizing specific experiences) and for the generalization of actions that take place primarily in the child's natural environment (e.g. working with parents, teachers, and peers; training beyond termination).

Ayelet was in therapy for a long period of time, and we directed therapy to her individual needs, family relationships, peers, and vocational and social behaviors. As we progressed, Ayelet had to experience eating out of the home, with other people, and she faced stress and difficulties while studying and as she started working. These multiple trials ensured us of her ability to maintain treatment outcomes without regression.

11

And Last But Not Least

I have tried to pinpoint features relating to a successful process of change – assessment and evaluation, decision making, emotional components, therapeutic relationships, theories, methods, and techniques. However, an effective process of change is based on more than techniques and methods. It requires a constant process of listening, understanding, checking, rechecking, doubting, and questioning. The question should continuously be asked in the therapist's mind: What is the most important thing I can do for this client, with this problem, at this moment? There is no one recipe for success, but I hope this inventory of ideas will contribute to therapists' continuous self-monitoring and planning of the active steps that should be performed in any therapeutic intervention.

PART VI

Closing Remarks

In writing this book, several motives spurred me to devote the requisite time and emotional energy in order to bring this multifaceted account of our therapeutic encounter to fruition. Personal incentives, professional motives, and social considerations intertwined, impelling me to undertake this endeavor.

My personal incentives relate to both Ayelet's and my own personal stories of this treatment. First, I believed that by complying with Ayelet's desire to tell her story, I would be making a significant contribution to her holistic, Gestalt closure of issues connected to her past. Ayelet felt that, in order for her to fully open herself up to a new life as a healthy, happy, content young woman, she needed, first of all, to finish dealing with her past. She wanted to tell her story, to more wholly understand herself and her behavior, and to ensure that she had indeed changed and could trust herself and her capability to live differently in the future. Second, as far as my own incentives go, I found myself drawn to the idea of professional writing that would be unique and particularly meaningful. Most of my writings over the years have been related to professional materials, professional considerations, and scientific knowledge. Here in this book, I hoped not only to relay my personal and professional experiences as Ayelet's therapist, but also to share this particular narrative. I feel her story is one that deserves sharing with others.

Treating Ayelet was a very different and unique experience for me. Although I generally espouse an approach that focuses on the person rather than the problem, it was particularly easy to relate to Ayelet in the human aspect, rather than only with the professional face of the therapist. When I ask myself in what way Ayelet challenged me, and made me feel different than I felt in other therapies, I think it might be related to several issues. First, Ayelet's story was very moving. She suffered greatly; she could not find her way out of her labyrinth of problems; she had a very long history of pain; and the manner in which she talked during sessions aroused much emotion. Second, she was very creative, and her usage of drawings, writings, and metaphoric language conveyed her feelings in a way that easily enabled me to feel tuned in to what she was discussing. Third, Ayelet posed a challenge in that she had undergone many previous therapies, and her very complexity summoned me to help her. Fourth, the contradiction between that complexity of her disorders, on the one hand, and the very impressive young woman I met, on the other, kindled my curiosity and wish to help her.

I often tell my students that the therapist's emotions after sessions are the best way to learn about the client's condition and the treatment process. With Ayelet, I always felt tired, involved, caring, and a combination of feelings that moved between fear and hope. As I treated her, I often felt I was crying and suffering with her. Often, it was not easy to maintain distance, to remain in my therapist's seat, and to refrain from approaching her and embracing her. For much of the time during her therapy, despite her abundant creative outlets for expression, Ayelet maintained distance during the sessions, both from her own emotions and from me. Thus, I found myself intensely experiencing feelings that she herself could not yet endure, and these feelings served us well as a tool for insight and for forging the bonds between thoughts, feelings, self-images, and personal interrelations.

Additional motives for writing this volume relate to professional interests. In treating Ayelet, I designed an intervention that could be adapted to her unique needs and personality. I did not use one prevalent technique or available method, but rather devised a comprehensive intervention package based on a cognitive-constructivist approach. Few descriptions of such interventions can be found, and I thought that cognitive-constructivist therapists as well as other professionals might benefit from reading this account.

Also, in this treatment I used a multiple baseline design and a multiple treatment design, which afforded me the ability to evaluate the progress of discrete treatment components. This unique multivariate design, with its possibilities for assessing and evaluating complex interventions, underscores my belief that every therapist should use methods to evaluate intervention processes and study their efficacy.

Another professional catalyst for this book was my hope to promote the flexible integration of personalized, creative, nonverbal techniques. As Kanfer and Schefft (1988) proposed, therapists should be flexible. I have no doubt that Ayelet's treatment clearly presents the need to carefully listen to the client's language, hobbies, and unique nature, as well as to attempt treatment methods that appear to optimally fit the client's needs and resources. Treating Ayelet involved a nonstop process of me asking myself what kinds of techniques could best suit my specific goals at that particular stage of therapy, especially which techniques could best help in mobilizing Ayelet's motivation and yearning for change. This book is peppered with some of the many metaphors, imagery and mirror techniques, role plays, written exercises, and verbal discussions that I employed.

Much material has been presented on theories of anorexia. Likewise, a number of books have relayed personal stories of anorexic persons. I believe this book is unique in the combination being offered – a vivid personal narrative from both parties' perspectives, along with the therapist's treatment considerations. This might contribute meaningfully to those interested in applying the treatment recommended herein.

And, last but not least, during the last few years anorexia has become a social problem. On the one hand, the media is ceaselessly confronting us with young, thin, good-looking models and actresses, and with new ways to diet and to achieve rapid weight loss. Being thin and dieting are strongly reinforced in all of the media. On the other hand, the educational as well as psychological and psychiatric settings are very concerned about the increase of anorexia. The frequency of the disorder is increasing, with younger and younger girls developing it. The life-endangering nature of this disorder places it at the forefront of public awareness. One can always find an article in the paper, a movie on television, or a book related to anorexia. While research outcomes are progressing related to the assessment, diagnosis, and treatment of adolescents, many debates continue concerning the efficacy of intervention and the selection of optimal therapies targeting anorexia.

I thought it worth focusing the attention not only of therapists, but also of parents, educators, counselors, and the anorexic girls themselves. Perhaps reading about the entire process, its pain and sorrow, as well as its improvement and success, might encourage others to give anorexia a second thought, to stop before it is too late, and to ask for therapy. I hope this book will help parents and adolescents alike to learn about these difficult problems, and perhaps will prevent some people's suffering.

Writing a book is a very stimulating, emotional process. With this book, even more so, because it involved a process of sharing and collaborating with Ayelet. It was a privilege to work with her over the years in therapy and in writing the book, and I am certain that her courage and perseverance will serve to inspire both therapists as well as young people who identify some of her in themselves.

Glossary

This Glossary is divided into four separate issues:

1. Diagnoses

2. Treatment Process

3. Therapies

4. Treatment Concepts.

Diagnoses

Anorexia Severe disturbances in eating behavior. Refusal to maintain body weight at or above a minimally normal weight for age and height. A decrease of 15 percent of body weight.

Borderline personality A pervasive pattern of instability of interpersonal relationships, self-image, and caring relationships, and marked impulsivity.

Depression A period of at least two weeks of a depressed mood, loss of interest or pleasure in nearly all activities. Loss of appetite or weight, sleep disturbances, decreased amount of energy and a feeling of worthlessness, thoughts of death.

DSM-IV A psychiatric manual (dictionary) that includes diagnostic and statistical criteria for mental disorders.

Eating disorders See *Anorexia*.

Encopresis A repeated passage of feces into inappropriate places. Most often this is involuntary but occasionally may be intentional, for at least three months, after the age of four.

Enuresis Repeated voiding of urine during the day or night into clothes or bed, with minimal frequency of twice a week for at least three months, after the age of four.

Externalizing disorders Behaviors acted outward toward the environment. Mainly related to disobedience, aggression, oppositional, or antisocial behaviors.

Intellectualization A process of giving oneself rational explanations and excuses for events. A term often used when someone avoids relating to emotional internal processes and finds the causes and justifications in rational explanation.

Internalizing disorders Behavior related mostly to emotional, internal processes, which causes distress to the person. Usually related to emotions such as fear, loneliness, and depression.

Obsessive-compulsive disorder (OCD) Obsession (persistent ideas, thoughts, and images) that causes marked anxiety or distress and/or compulsions (repetitive behaviors or mental acts) that serve to neutralize the anxiety.

Oppositional defiant disorders One of the diagnoses relating to childhood conduct disorders. Related mainly to a recurrent pattern of negativistic, defiant, disobedient, and hostile behavior toward authority figures, persisting for at least six months.

Personality disorders An enduring pattern of inner experience and behavior that deviates markedly from the expectations of the individual culture, is pervasive and inflexible, and leads to distress or impairment.

Somatic disorders The presence of physical symptoms that suggest a general medical condition, but are not fully explained by a general medical condition. Must cause clinically significant distress or impairment in social, occupational, or other areas.

Suicidal personality A propensity to commit suicide (or attempt), usually related to depression and to a negative view of the world and oneself.

Treatment Process

Baseline data Relating to how the client behaves (feels or thinks) before starting therapy.

Compliance The willingness of the client to adhere and comply with the treatment assignments and exercises.

Intervention process Involves a series of sessions for resolving problems and includes well accepted steps such as getting acquainted, designing a good alliance and therapeutic relationship, working together toward change, practicing exercises, termination, maintenance, and evaluation of treatment outcomes.

Problem areas A concept relating to behavior therapy that points to the need to list all the problems from which the client suffers and to divide them into similar areas.

Therapies

Behavior therapy A psychotherapy based on learning theory. Emphasis is on the present as the target of change. Views behavior as results from the behavior's consequence and change as an outcome of giving positive reward to the wishful behavior. Focuses on applying skills to enable change.

Cognitive therapy A psychotherapy based on the link between thoughts, emotions, and behaviors. Views human disorder as something that has been learned and maintained by the way the individual thinks and conceives of life. Focuses on teaching ways to change automatic thoughts and applying skills for change.

Constructivism A psychotherapy based on the subjective way in which human beings conceive and conceptualize their lives. Emphasizes how people attribute meaning into their lives. Focuses on challenging clients to open up to experiences, experiment, explore, and give new meaning to their lives.

Family therapy A psychotherapy based on viewing the family as the main setting in which people live, and therefore as responsible for the development of disorder. Focuses on changing roles and communication styles within the family.

Psychoanalysis A psychotherapy developed by Sigmund Freud, emphasizing the first year of life as responsible for the client's disorders. Focuses on insight as the most important element in the process of change.

Treatment Concepts

Automatic or unmediated thought A concept from cognitive therapy relating to the automatic, unmediated tendency of human beings to interpret events as responsible for their distress.

Avoidance behavior A behavior of stopping, regressing, or inhibiting responses in order to stop anxiety.

Belief system A concept related to cognitive therapy. Viewed as an important feature of the development and maintenance of a disorder, and as an important target for change in order to overcome difficulties.

Collaboration A mutual work agreement between client and therapist for achieving the goals of therapy.

Countertransference The kind of relations and feelings developed in the psychoanalytical therapist toward his or her client.

Deficient behavior A concept used with reference to under-controlled behavior. Describes children who lack appropriate skills for controlling their behavior.

Distorted thinking A concept used to describe children suffering from over-controlled behavior, who set overly high expectations and criteria for their achievement.

Empowerment A process of reinforcing and challenging clients for independent functioning. Focuses on developing resources and skills for self-change.

Experiencing A major concept of constructivist therapy. Emphasizes the importance of trying new or different experiences in order to develop and change.

Experimentation Another major concept from constructivist therapy. Views human beings as scientists who should try to study and experiment with the way they behave, think, and feel.

Exploring The third concept of this group of constructivist concepts, along with experiencing and experimenting. Relates to the need to open up to experiences, be curious and learn new things about the world and oneself.

Maladaptive perception (or misconception) A way of thinking that develops that hinders a person's functioning. Not belonging to reality but to a personal conceptualization of event that causes distress and pain.

Meaning-making process A constructivist concept relating to the subjective way in which the person, rather than the objective reality, is responsible for the disorder.

Over-controlled behavior Possessing the needed skills to act, but establishing overly high expectations, goals, or criteria, and therefore developing distress. Usually related to disorders such as depression and anxiety.

Schema A concept from cognitive therapy. Relates to the basic core ideas that have developed since childhood, including automatic thoughts, belief system and self-talk. It presents one's views of the world or of oneself.

Self-acceptance The ability of human beings to like, live in peace with, and feel good with themselves as they are.

Self-confidence Similar to self-acceptance. The ability to trust oneself and dare to do things and face challenges.

Self-evaluation The ability to appreciate oneself as a worthy human being, or the process of monitoring and assessing oneself.

Transference A concept from psychoanalytic theory that views the therapeutic relationship as a model for transferring other kinds of relationships held by the client (for example, parental relationships).

Techniques

Attentional focus Used in cognitive and constructivist therapy for increasing the client's awareness of internal stimuli and cues.

Cognitive restructuring (structuring) Cognitive technique for helping the client change his or her way of thinking and constructs new way for conceptualizing the world.

Collaboration efforts The mutual efforts of client and therapist to work together and cooperate toward the goal of change.

Continuum methods A cognitive method of comparing oneself to other people, situations or events, in order to increase self-evaluation and self-acceptance.

Desensitization A behavioral technique developed by Wolpe. Uses relaxation and imagination in combination with the feared event to gradually decrease sensitization that elicits anxiety.

Evaluation circle Helps establish how clients view themselves by looking at what they believe others think of them. The circle is represented by sets of the people we know in our social environment – the closest circle is made up of our immediate family, good friends can be another circle, etc.

Experiential techniques All the techniques used to challenge the client to try and do things that might help him or her change concepts and behavior.

Exposure A behavioral technique for decreasing fear and anxiety, based on assignments that gradually face clients with feared events.

Homework assignments Behavioral and cognitive technique for giving exercises to the client to carry out at home. Aims to generalize treatment outcomes, maintain the achieved change, and facilitate progress.

Imagery Used in behavioral, cognitive, and constructivist therapy to utilize images for helping the client change. Can be a preliminary exercise before exposure to real-life situations or can be a therapy itself.

Increasing awareness See *Attentional focus.*

Maintenance Preserving the treatment outcome and avoiding regression after the change process.

Metaphor A constructivist technique for helping the client change via use of images taken from another situation. Gives clients more vivid examples or demonstrration of their problems or a way to change problems.

Mirror time A constructivist exercise that employs talking, sitting, and acting in front of the mirror as a way to achieve change, self-acceptance.

Modeling A technique from learning theory in which the client learns from viewing or appreciating someone else's behavior (model).

Premark principle A concept taken from learning theory which explains how one can be persuaded to do something one is not interested in doing by conditioning it to an activity that one wishes to do.

Redefinition (reframing) A way to organize the client's thinking in a new way that is more positive and facilitates change.

Rehearsal A behavioral technique helping clients rehearse and practice the skills needed ahead.

Reinforcements A behavioral technique that aims to increase desired behavior by giving the client a reward after accomplishing this behavior.

Relaxation A behavioral technique that aims to teach clients a method for decreasing anxiety.

Resourcefulness A cognitive concept taken from self-control therapy. Relates to skills one can learn to help oneself cope.

Self-control training A cognitive technique that aims to teach clients skills for self-help.

Self-instruction, self-talk A cognitive technique for changing automatic, negative thoughts by use of positive verbalization or giving oneself instructions.

Self-monitoring The process of teaching clients to identify their behavior by observing themselves, and to record and chart their progress.

Self-observation A cognitive-behavioral technique that comprises part of the self-monitoring process, where behaviors are observed and then recorded.

Self-rewards A cognitive-behavioral technique teaching clients to reinforce themselves as a way of increasing self-control.

Skills acquisition A treatment process that imparts to clients the necessary lacking skills.

Social skills training A method for increasing skills for social relationships via training.

References

Achenbach, T. M. (1985) *Assessment and taxonomy of child and adolescent psychopathology.* Beverly Hills: Sage.

Alford, B. A. and Beck, A. T. (1997) *The integrative power of cognitive therapy.* New York: Guilford Press.

American Psychiatric Association (1994) *Diagnostic and statistical manual of mental disorders* (DSM; 4th edition). Washington, DC: Author.

Bailey, V. (1998) 'Conduct disorders in young children.' In P. Graham (ed) *Cognitive behaviour therapy with children and families.* Cambridge: Cambridge University Press.

Bandura, A. (1969) *Principles of behavior modification.* New York: Holt, Rinehart & Winston.

Bandura, A. (1977) *Social learning theory.* Englewood Cliffs, NJ: Prentice Hall.

Bandura, A. (1997) *Self-efficacy: The exercise of control.* New York: W. H. Freeman.

Barkley, R.A. (1997) 'Behavioural inhibition, sustained attention and executive functions: Constructing unifying theory of ADHD.' *Psychological Bulletin 121,* 65–94.

Barrios, B. A. and Hartman, D. P. (1988) 'Fears and anxieties.' In E. J. Mash and L. G. Terdal (eds) *Behavioral assessment of childhood disorders.* New York: Guilford Press.

Beck, A. T. (1963) 'Thinking and depression.' *Archives of General Psychiatry, 9,* 324–333.

Beck, A. T. (1976) *Cognitive therapy and the emotional disorders.* New York: Meridian.

Beck, A. T., Emery, G. and Greenberg, R. L. (1985) *Anxiety disorders and phobias: A cognitive perspective.* New York: Basic Books.

Beck, A. T., Freeman, A. and Associates (1990) *Cognitive therapy of personality disorders.* New York: Guilford Press.

Beck, A. T., Rush, A. J., Shaw, B. F. and Emery, G. (1979) *Cognitive therapy of depression.* New York: Guilford Press.

Brandell, J. R. (1992) 'Psychotherapy of a traumatized 10-year-old boy: Theroretical issues and clinical observations.' *Smith College Studies in Social Work 62, 2, 123–138.*

Brigham, T. A., Hopper, A. J., Shaw, B. F. and Emery, G. (1979) *Cognitive therapy of depression.* New York: Guilford Press.

Bruch, H. (1973) *Eating disorders: Obesity, anorexia, and the person within.* New York: Basic Books.

Bruch, H. (1977) 'Psychological antecedents of anorexia nervosa.' In R. A. Vigersky (ed) *Anorexia nervosa.* New York: Raven Press.

Bruch, H. (1986) 'Anorexia nervosa: The therapeutic task.' In K. D. Brownell and J. P. Foreyt (eds) *Handbook of eating disorders: Physiology, psychology, and treatment of obesity, anorexia, and bulimia.* New York: Basic Books.

Bugental, J. F. T. (1987) *The art of the psychotherapist.* New York: Norton.

Clarkson, P. (1995) *The therapeutic relationships.* London: Whurr Publishers.

Crisp, A. H. (1980) *Anorexia nervosa: Let me be.* London: Plenum Press.

Dally, P. (1969) *Anorexia nervosa.* New York: Grune & Stratton.

Dare, C. and Crowther, C. (1995) 'Psychodynamic models of eating disorders.' In G. Szmukler, C. Dare and J. Treasure (eds) *Handbook of eating disorders: Theory, treatment and research.* Chichester, UK: Wiley.

Dare, C. and Eisler, I. (1995) 'Family therapy.' In G. Szmukler, C. Dare and J. Treasure (eds) *Handbook of eating disorders: Theory, treatment and research.* Chichester, UK: Wiley.

Dare, C. and Key, A. (1999) 'Family functioning and adolescent anorexia nervosa.' *British Journal of Psychiatry 175,* 1999–2009.

Durlak, J. A., Fuhrman, T. and Lampman, C. (1991) 'Effectiveness of cognitive-behavior therapy for maladaptive children: A meta-analysis.' *Psychological Bulletin 110,* 204–214.

Eisler, I. (1995) 'Family models of eating disorders.' In G. Szmukler, C. Dare and J. Treasure (eds) *Handbook of eating disorders: Theory, treatment and research.* Chichester, UK: Wiley.

Elias, M. J., Gara, M., Ubriaco, M., Rothbaum, P., Clabby, J. F. and Schuyler, T. (1986) 'Impact of a preventive social problem solving intervention on children's coping with middle stressors.' *American Journal of Community Psychology 14,* 259–275.

Ellis, A. (1962) *Reason and emotion in psychotherapy.* New York: Lyle Stuart.

Fairburn, C. G., Shafran, R. and Cooper, Z. (1999) 'A cognitive behavioral theory of anorexia nervosa.' *Behavior Research and Therapy 37,* 1–13.

Finch, A.J., Nelson, W.M. and Ott, E.S. (1993) *Cognitive bahavioral procedures with children and adolescents: A practicle guide.* Boston: Allyn and Bacon.

Foreyt, J. P. and McGavin, J. K. (1988) 'Anorexia nervosa and bulimia.' In E. J. Mash and L. G. Terdal (eds) *Behavioral assessment of childhood disorders* (2nd edition). New York: Guilford Press.

Foster, S. L. and Robin, A. L. (1988) 'Family conflict and communication in adolescence.' In E. J. Mash and L. G. Terdal (eds) *Behavioral assessment of childhood disorders.* New York: Guilford Press.

Freeman, C. (1995) 'Cognitive therapy.' In G. Szmukler, C. Dare and J. Treasure (eds) *Handbook of eating disorders: Theory, treatment and research.* Chichester, UK: Wiley.

Gambrill, E. D. (1990) *Critical thinking in clinical practice.* San Francisco: Jossey-Bass.

Gambrill, E. D., Thomas, E. J. and Carter, R. D. (1971) 'Procedure for sociobehavioral practice in open settings.' *Social Work, 16,* 51–62.

Garner, D. M. (1986) 'Cognitive therapy for anorexia nervosa.' In K. D. Brownell and J. P. Foreyt (eds) *Handbook of eating disorders.* New York: Basic Books.

Greenberg, L.S. and Saffran, J.D. (1987) *Emotion in psychotherapy.* New York: Guildford Press.

Gowers, S. and North, C. (1999) 'Family functioning and adolescent anorexia nervosa.' *British Journal of Psychiatry, 175,* 89–90.

Guidano, V. F. (1995) 'Constructivist psychotherapy: A theoretical framework.' In R. A. Neimeyer and M. J. Mahoney (eds) *Constructivism in psychotherapy* Washington DC: American Psychological Association.

Guidano, V. F. and Liotti, G. (1983) *Cognitive processes and emotional disorders.* New York: Guilford Press.

Halmi, K. A. (1995) 'Current concepts and definitions.' In G. Szmukler, C. Dare and J. Treasure (eds) *Handbook of eating disorders: Theory, treatment and research.* Chichester, UK: Wiley.

Hamama, R., Ronen, T. and Feigin, R. (2000) 'Self-control, anxiety and loneliness in siblings of children with cancer.' *Social Work in Health Care, 31,* 63–83.

Hayes, S.C., Jacobson, N.S., Folette, V.M. and Doughter, M.J. (1994) *Acceptance and change: Content and context in psychotherapy.* New York: Context Press.

Herbert, M. (1987) (2nd edition) *Conduct disorders of childhood and adolscence: A social learning perpective.* Chichester: Wiley.

Hersen, M. and Bellack, A. S. (1981) *Behavioral assessment.* New York: Pergamon Press.

Hollon, S. D. and Beck, A. T. (1994) 'Cognitive and cognitive behavioral therapies.' In A. E. Bergin and S. L. Garfield (eds) *Handbook of psychotherapy and behavior change.* (4th edition) New York: Guilford Press.

Hops, H. and Greenwood, C. R. (1988) 'Social skill deficits.' In E. J. Mash and L. G. Terdal (eds) *Behavioral assessment of childhood disorders* (pp.263–314). New York: Guilford Press.

Joyce, J. (1980) *Finnegan's wake.* London: Faber & Faber.

Kanfer, F. H. and Philips, J. S. (1970) *Learning foundation of behavior therapy.* New York: Wiley.

Kanfer, F. H. and Schefft, B. K. (1988) *Guiding the process of therapeutic change.* Champaign, IL: Research Press.

Kazdin, A.E. (1987) *Conduct disorders in childhood and adolescence.* Newbury Park, CA: Sage.

Karoly, P. and Kanfer, F. H. (eds) (1982) *Self-management and behavior change. From theory to practice.* New York: Pergamon Press.

Kazdin, A. E. (1982) *Single-case research design: Methods for clinical and applied settings.* New York: Oxford University Press.

Kazdin, A. E. (1988) *Child psychotherapy: Developing and identifying effective treatments.* New York: Pergamon Press.

Kelly, G. A. (1955) *The psychology of personal constructs.* New York: Norton.

Kendall, P. C. (1985) 'Toward a cognitive-behavioral model of child psychopathology and a critique of related interventions.' *Journal of Abnormal Child Psychology, 13,* 357–372.

Kendall, P. C. (1994) 'Treating anxiety disorders in youth: Results of a randomized trial.' *Journal of Consulting and Clinical Psychology, 62*, 100–110.

Kendall, P. C. and Braswell, L. (1985) *Cognitive-behavioral therapy for impulsive children.* New York: Guilford Press.

Kendall, P. C. and Hollon, S. D. (eds) (1979) *Cognitive-behavioral interventions: Theory, research, and procedures.* New York: Academic Press.

Kopp, R. R. (1995) *Metaphor therapy: Using client-generated metaphors in psychotherapy.* New York: Brunner/Mazel.

Lazarus, R. S. (1984) 'On the primacy of cognition.' *American Psychologist 39*, 124–129.

Mahoney, M. J. (1977) 'Reflections on the cognitive learning trend in psychotherapy.' *American Psychologist 32*, 5–13.

Mahoney, M. J. (1991) *Human change process: The scientific foundations of psychotherapy.* New York: Basic Books.

Mahoney, M. J. (1993) 'Introduction to special section: Theoretical developments in the cognitive psychotherapies.' *Journal of Consulting and Clinical Psychology, 61*, 187–193.

Mahoney, M. J. (1995) 'Continuing evolution of the cognitive science and psychotherapies.' In R. A. Neimeyer and M. J. Mahoney (eds) *Constructivism in psychotherapy.* Washington, DC: American Psychological Association.

Mair, M. (1988) 'Psychology as storytelling.' *International Journal of Personal Construct Psychology 1*, 125–137.

Marks, I. (1969) *Fears and phobias.* New York: Academic Press.

Marks, I. (1978) *Living with fear.* New York: McGraw-Hill.

Marks, I. (1987) *Fears, phobias and rituals.* New York: Oxford University Press.

Meichenbaum, D. H. (1979) 'Teaching children self-control.' In B. Lahey and A. Kazdin (eds) *Advances in clinical child psychology* (Vol. 2). New York: Plenum.

Meichenbaum, D. H. and Turk, D. C. (1987) *Facilitating treatment adherence: A practitioner's guidebook.* New York: Plenum.

Minuchin, S., Baker, L., Liebman, R., Milman, L. and Todd, T. C. (1975) 'A conceptual model of psychosomatic illness in children.' *Archives of General Psychiatry 32*, 1031–1038.

Minuchin, S., Rossman, B. L. and Baker, L. (1978) *Psychosomatic families: Anorexia nervosa in context.* Cambridge, MA: Harvard University Press.

Neimeyer, R. A. (1995) 'Constructivist psychotherapies: Features, foundations, and future directions.' In R. A. Neimeyer and M. J. Mahoney (eds) *Constructivism in psychotherapy.* Washington, DC: American Psychological Association.

Neimeyer, R. A. and Mahoney, M. J. (eds) (1995) *Constructivism in psychotherapy.* Washington, DC: American Psychological Association.

Palla, B. and Litt, I. (1988) 'Medical complications of eating disorders in adolescents.' *Pediatrics 81*, 613–623.

Parker, R.D. (1994) 'Progress, paradigms and unresolved problems: Recent advances in our understanding of children's emotions.' *Merria-Palmer Quarterly 40,* 157–169.

Powell, M. B. and Oei, T. P. S. (1991) 'Cognitive processes underlying the behavior change in cognitive behavior therapy with childhood disorders: A review of experimental evidence.' *Behavioral Psychotherapy 19,* 247–265.

Rachman, S. (1997) 'A cognitive theory of obsessions.' *Behavior Research and Therapy, 35* 793–802.

Robin, A.L. (1985) 'Parent adolescent conflict: A developmental problem of families.' In R.J. McMahon and R. Dev Peters (eds) *Childhood disorders.* New York: Bruner/Mazel.

Robin, A. L. and Siegel, P. T. (1999) 'Family therapy with eating disordered adolescents.' In R. S. Walker and T. H. Ollendick (eds) *Handbook of psychotherapies with children and families.* New York: Kluwer/Plenum.

Ronan, K. R. and Deane, F. P. (1998) 'Anxiety disorders.' In P. Graham (ed) *Cognitive-behaviour therapy for children and families.* Cambridge: Cambridge University Press.

Ronan, K. R. and Kendall, P. C. (1991) 'Non-self-controlled adolescents: Applications of cognitive-behavioral therapy.' In S. C. Feinstein (ed) *Adolescent psychiatry: Developmental and clinical studies.* Chicago: University of Chicago Press.

Ronen, T. (1992) 'Cognitive Therapy with young children.' *Child Psychiatry and Human Development 23,* 1, 19–30.

Ronen, T. (1993a) 'Self-control training in the treatment of sleep-terror disorders.' *Child and Family Behavior Therapy 15,* 53–63.

Ronen, T. (1993b) 'Intervention package for treating encopresis in a six-year-old boy.' *Behavioural Psychotherapy 27,* 127–135.

Ronen, T. (1994) 'Imparting self-control in a school setting.' *Child and Family Behavior Therapy 16,* 1–20.

Ronen, T. (1995) 'From what kind of self control can children benefit?' *The Journal of Cognitive Psychotherapy: An International Quarterly 9,* 45–61.

Ronen, T. (1996) 'Self-control exposure therapy for treating children's anxieties.' *Child and Family Behavior Therapy 18,* 1–17.

Ronen, T. (1997a) 'Cognitive-behavioural therapy.' In M. Davies (ed) *The Blackwell companion to social work.* Oxford: Blackwell.

Ronen, T. (1997b) *Cognitive developmental therapy with children.* Chichester, UK: Wiley.

Ronen, T. (1998) 'Linking developmental and emotional elements into child and family cognitive behavioral therapy.' In P. Graham (ed) *Cognitive-behaviour therapy for children and families.* Cambridge: Cambridge University Press.

Ronen, T. (in press) *Using creative techniques in cognitive psychotherapy with children and adolescents.* Northvale, NJ: Jason Aronson.

Ronen, T. and Rosenbaum, M. (1998) 'Beyond verbal instruction in cognitive behavioral supervision.' *Cognitive and Behavioral Practice 5,* 3–19.

Ronen, T. and Rosenbaum, M. (in press) 'Helping children to help themselves: A case study of enuresis and nail biting.' *Research in Social Work Practice.*

Ronen, T. and Wozner, Y. (1995) 'A self-control intervention package for elimination of enuresis.' *Child and Family Behavior Therapy 17*, 1–20.

Ronen, T., Wozner, Y. and Rahav, G. (1995) 'Self-control and enuresis.' *The Journal of Cognitive Psychotherapy: An International Quarterly 9*, 4, 249–258.

Rose, S.D. and Edelson, J. L. (1988) *Working with children and adolescents in groups.* San Francisco: Jossey-Bass.

Rosenbaum, M. (1993) 'The three functions of self-control behavior: Redressive, reformative and experiential.' *Journal of Work and Stress, 7*, 33–46.

Rosenbaum, M. (1999) 'The self-regulation of experience: Openness and construction.' In D. Dewe, T. Cox and A. M. Leiter (eds) *Coping, health and organizations.* London: Taylor & Francis.

Rosenbaum, M. and Ronen, T. (1998) 'Clinical supervision from the standpoint of cognitive-behavior therapy.' *Psychotherapy, 35*, 220–229.

Russell, G. F. M. (1995) 'Anorexia nervosa through time.' In G. Szmukler, C. Dare and J. Treasure (eds) *Handbook of eating disorders: Theory, treatment and research.* Chichester, UK: Wiley.

Safran, J. D. and Segal, Z. V. (1990) *Interpersonal process in cognitive therapy.* New York: Basic Books.

Salkovskis, P. M. (1996) 'Cognitive-behavioral approaches to the understanding of obsessional problems.' In R. Rapee (ed) *Current controversies in anxiety disorders.* New York: Guilford Press.

Schmidt, U. (1998) 'Eating disorders and obesity.' In P. Graham (ed) *Cognitive-behaviour therapy for children and families.* Cambridge: Cambridge University Press.

Shafran, R. (1998) 'Childhood obsessive-compulsive disorder.' In P. Graham (ed) *Cognitive-behaviour therapy for children and families.* Cambridge: Cambridge University Press.

Shirk, S.R. and Russell, R.L. (1996) *Change process in child psychotherapy.* New York: Guildford Press.

Siegel, L. J. and Smith, K. E. (1991) 'Somatic disorders.' In T. R. Kratochwill and R. J. Morris (eds) *The practice of child therapy.* New York: Pergamon Press.

Silverman, J. A. (1995) 'Something new under the sun: Comments on Gerald Russell's "Anorexia nervosa through time".' In G. Szmukler, C. Dare and J. Treasure (eds) *Handbook of eating disorders: Theory, treatment and research.* Chichester, UK: Wiley.

Strober, M. (1980) 'A cross-sectional and longitudinal analysis of personality and symptomological features in young non-chronic anorexia nervosa patients.' *Journal of Psychosomatic Research 24*, 353–359.

Swell, K. W. (1996) 'Constructional risk factors for post-traumatic stress response after a mass murder.' *Journal of Constructivist Psychology 9*, 97–107.

Terworgt, M.M. and Olthof, T. (1989) 'Awareness and self-regulation of emotion in young children.' In C. Saarni and P.L Harris (eds) *Children's understanding of emotion.* New York: Cambridge University Perss.

Theander, A. S. (1995) 'The essence of anorexia nervosa: Comment on Gerald Russell's "Anorexia nervosa through time".' In G. Szmukler, C. Dare and J.

Treasure (eds) *Handbook of eating disorders: Theory, treatment and research.* Chichester, UK: Wiley.

Thompson, R. A. and Sherman, R. T. (1999) '"Good athlete" traits and characteristics of anorexia nervosa: Are they similar?' *Eating Disorder: The Journal of Treatment and Prevention 7,* 181–190.

Thoresen, C. E. and Mahoney, M. J. (1974) *Behavioral self-control.* New York: Holt, Rinehart & Winston.

Thyer, B. A. (1991) 'Diagnosis and treatment of child and adolescent anxiety disorders.' *Behavior Modification 15,* 310–325.

Thyer, B. A. and Sowers-Hoag, K. M. (1988) 'Behavior therapy for separation anxiety disorder of childhood.' *Behavior Modification 12,* 205–233.

Vitousek, K. B. and Hollon, K. B. (1990) 'The investigation of schematic content and processing in eating disorders.' *Cognitive Therapy and Research 14,* 191–214.

Ward, A., Troop, N., Todd, G. and Treasure, J. (1996) 'To change or not to change: How is the question?' *British Journal of Medical Psychology 69,* 139–146.

Weisberg, R. W. (1992) 'Metacognition and insight during problem solving.' *Journal of experimental psychology: Learning, memory and cognition 18,* 426–431.

Williamson, D. A., Miller, S. L., Reas, D. L. and Thaw, J. M. (1999) 'Cognitive bias in eating disorders: Implications for theory and treatment.' *Behavior Modification 23,* 556–577.

Wilson, G. T., Heffernan, K. and Black, C. M. D. (1996) 'Eating disorders.' In E. J. Mash and R. A. Barkley (eds) *Child psychopathology.* New York: Guilford Press.

Wozner, Y. (1985) *Behavior change.* Tel-Aviv: Papirus University Press.

Subject Index

Author Index